PRAISE FOR
20 WOMEN CHANGEMAKERS

"There is nothing more inspiring to me than to **hear the stories of women from around the world, leading from a place of confidence and purpose to create change.** These are truly extraordinary women, who through their work, teach us all something new and inspire me to roll up my sleeves to do more."

  —Pernille Spiers-Lopez
   Former President of IKEA North America
   Author of *Design Your Life*

"**Phenomenal women, doing extraordinary work, captured through remarkable narratives.** From change-makers to game-changers, defying the odds to rise above the mundane—this is what our world so desperately longs for. This is what *The Women's Eye* brings to light. I am absolutely inspired by the strength and compassion that come through every single pursuit of purpose brought out by **this outstanding compilation.**"

  —Umra Omar, Founder of Safari Doctors
   CNN Hero

"Pamela Burke of *The Women's Eye* has compiled **the best of her wonderful and inspiring interviews of women who are changing the world**—from Jessica Posner, who built the first free school for girls in Kenya, to Jenny Bowen, who is providing better lives for abandoned girls in China; from women working to support the homeless to those helping others through grief. I came away with a renewed sense of wanting to do and be more."

> —**Lisa See,** New York Times Bestselling
> Author of *Snow Flower and the Secret Fan,*
> *Shanghai Girls, Dreams of Joy* and *China Dolls*

"*The Women's Eye* has put together **a handbook for social justice and activism guaranteed to lift spirits and inform ideals.** *20 Women Changemakers* are ordinary women who found their passion to do extraordinary things. They share tips on how they achieved their goals, along with websites to connect with them and their causes and book club discussion questions to challenge every reader."

> —**Eleanor Clift**
> Washington Correspondent, *The Daily Beast*

The Women's Eye Spotlights

20 WOMEN
CHANGEMAKERS

TAKING ACTION
AROUND THE WORLD

The Women's Eye Spotlights

20 WOMEN
CHANGEMAKERS

TAKING ACTION
AROUND THE WORLD

EDITED BY PAMELA BURKE
AND PATRICIA CASO

THE WOMEN'S EYE

For media and permission requests, contact the publisher at the website below.

www.thewomenseye.com

ISBN: 978-0-9977054-5-4

Printed in the United States of America

Edited by:
Pamela Burke and Patricia Caso
Cover and interior design by Jim Shubin—BookAlchemist.net

*To all the women who have contributed
to The Women's Eye and their dedication
to making a difference.*

Contents

Acknowledgments

The people who have worked with me on The Women's Eye book, website and radio program are some of the most talented and compassionate that I have known in the media world.

My co-editor and longtime friend Patricia Caso has been an extraordinary help in all aspects of TWE and this anthology. I so appreciate her time and effort in contacting our interviewees and working with them to gather the necessary information needed to assemble this book. She has also been a dedicated contributor, finding and interviewing several of our agents of change.

We want to thank the other contributors to this book, including the hard-working reporters who have interviewed these dedicated women. Hats off to Stacey Gualandi and Catherine Anaya, hosts of *The Women's Eye Radio Show* and both excellent journalists and broadcasters. We are grateful to Farzana Ali, who conducts interviews for TWE in Pakistan, and Amy Ernst, who reported for us from the Congo.

Some of these interviews were recorded on *The Women's Eye Radio Show* at 1480 KPHX in Phoenix,

Arizona. We thank Jonathan Molina, Eric Reinert and Kathleen Osborn for their continuing contribution and support for us at that station.

We salute the independent bookstores that hold numerous author events where we have been able to meet and learn about some of our intrepid subjects. A big thanks goes to the folks at Changing Hands Bookstore in Phoenix, Arizona, including Brandon Stout, Director of Marketing; and Book Passage in Corte Madera, California, and Sam Barry, Author Services Liaison, for their assistance and the care they take to present interesting writers. We couldn't do this book without the assistance also of our contacts at various publishing houses and we thank them.

Our own publishing team has been invaluable, giving us the tools and encouragement to make this dream of a book into a reality. We must thank Laurie McAndish King and Jim Shubin for their expertise and enthusiasm for this project.

Thanks also go to all the folks who have helped build and maintain The Women's Eye website. The talented Cheryl McLaughlin worked tirelessly to design the site, make it operational and keep it up to date. Ellen Laux, Andi Burnham and Garrett Miller have been tremendously helpful in maintaining it and spending the hours that it takes to have it function properly.

And lastly, we thank all the women whom we have met along the way who have allowed us into their lives so that we might spread their word and vision. They are changing the world in tremendous ways and we are grateful for them.

—Pamela Burke

Introduction

How exciting it is to be able to present the stellar group of changemakers who are in this anthology! You may have heard of some, but most labor in their missions without much acclaim. They live in countries all around the world but have this in common—commitment to positive change and to making the world a better place.

We highlight 20 remarkable people and their efforts to find solutions to some of our pressing global issues and to improve lives through their initiative. Our subjects' goals are sometimes daunting and certainly wide-ranging. They build schools where there were none, promote global women's issues in treacherous places and uncover ingenious new ways to feed the hungry, rescue children and more.

— From her house on Staten Island, New York, **Elissa Montanti** finds injured young people from around the world and brings them hope and much-needed medical care. Her first office was in her closet.

— From the interior of an old school bus, **Estella Pyfrom** bridges the digital divide, bringing modern technology to more than 31,000 underserved people.

— From a freezing cold kitchen in Beirut, **Barbara Massaad** came up with the idea to make and bring nourishing soup to Syrian refugees starving in tents in eastern Lebanon.

— From a dangerous slum in Kenya and a destitute valley in Nepal, **Jessica Posner** and **Maggie Doyne** bring groundbreaking schools to their desperate communities.

— From their homes in the U.S., **Jenny Bowen** and **Jerrie Ueberle** journey to China to save the lives of orphans and advance the opportunities of young women.

— From portable cardboard homes, walks through downtrodden neighborhoods and retrofitted buses, **Tina Hovsepian, Dr. Roseanna Means** and **Doniece Sandoval** find their solutions for helping the less fortunate.

Some of our changemakers saw tremendous voids and were determined to fill them. Film producer **Holly Gordon** wanted to call attention to the importance of valuing girls all over the world and produced the award-winning documentary "Girl Rising."

In light of the extraordinary accomplishments of grandmothers everywhere, **Paola Gianturco** traveled the globe to document them.

Helping poverty-stricken women and girls internationally became a number one priority for **Marsha Wallace**, founder of Dining for Women. How she has been able to achieve her vision is another one of TWE's amazing success stories.

And how do we find some of these intrepid women? Our contributor in northern Pakistan, Farzana Ali, told us about the miraculous peacebuilding efforts of **Gulalai Ismail** and her Aware Girls organization in that volatile part of the world. She talks about working for peace and prosperity no matter the risk.

We discovered contributor Amy Ernst in Congo, having transported herself there from Chicago to help COPERMA, a non-profit organization founded by **Maman Marie Nzoli**. This unsung hero assists victims of war and survivors of unspeakable sexual violence. She inspired Amy, and Amy inspires us with Maman's dedication to her cause.

We were fortunate to attend cancer survivor **Lauren Daniels'** Fairy Tale Tea in Phoenix, Arizona. There she paid tribute to the hundreds of volunteers who supported her for HEAL—the Happily Ever After

League—which she founded to help moms like herself with the overwhelming and costly challenges of cancer.

By attending various bookstore events, we have come across many proactive authors who write and speak from their own personal circumstances and heartache to help others cope. We were struck by how they are changing lives with their inspiring words. **Scarlett Lewis, Sukey Forbes** and **Jane Heller** opened our eyes to situations you might identify with when reading their stories.

Patty Chang Anker, author of *Some Nerve: Lessons Learned While Becoming Brave*, whom we met while producing our radio program, has a unique cause—a commitment to helping people face their fears. Like many of these women, Patty inspires us to be courageous, to embrace the challenges of the world and to stare fear in the face.

Why these particular women? That's a bit of a long story that we'll try to condense here. When I started The Women's Eye website, I was in search of positive stories about women. At the time, back in 2010, it seemed that we, in America, were adrift—trying to recover from a deadly recession.

Many disparate forces were afoot, including financial uncertainty and high unemployment rates.

With a background in television production and print journalism, my instincts were to find the positive side of this negative situation. I wanted to believe that there were people out there searching for solutions and new arenas of opportunity, and who were reaching out to improve the world in spite of the challenging circumstances.

I also saw the emergence of a growing new tech-based society and a rapid change in the distribution of information. I was motivated to try something new: to figure out how to use the power of the internet to spread stories of optimism, triumph, mission and purpose.

Women's topics have always interested me, not that men's haven't, but I felt a real need to pursue stories with a female voice as they were not getting the attention and the exposure that I thought they deserved.

With that premise, *The Women's Eye* emerged. Now, all these years later, we have been able to do interviews with and cover hundreds of stories about outstanding women whose accomplishments are making the world a global community of sharing and positive purpose.

We have compiled excerpts from interviews featured on *The Women's Eye Radio Show* and website in this anthology. There are more to share, but we felt we had to start somewhere.

We have witnessed a growing desire among women to speak up, to take the reins of their own destiny for the good of themselves and of the planet. They are wanting to solve the problems of the world rather than witness them. Change is afoot. We applaud it and want to support their positive action however we can. We hope you will, too.

As Patty Chang Anker says, "Our big goal, whether that's to learn to swim or write a book, will be challenging and we'll need all the courage and commitment we have. We need to decide once— and only once—to do it and then take what- ever obstacles that come as problems to be solved, not reasons to derail us."

Thanks for the encouragement Patty.

Here is our book!

　　—Pamela Burke
　　—Patricia Caso

Part I:
Taking Action Globally

"Never doubt that a small group of thoughtful, committed citizens can change the world; indeed, it's the only thing that ever has."

—*Margaret Mead*, Anthropologist

Jessica Posner

Jessica Posner on Building the First Free School for Girls in a Kenyan Slum

By Pamela Burke

Jessica Posner is doing extraordinary things in a place called Kibera, Kenya. It's the largest slum in Africa with 1.5 million people living in squalid conditions lacking running water and electricity. Most of the 500,000 girls under 18 in Kibera don't get the chance to go to school. But Jessica is making it her mission to provide free education for as many of them as she can.

Starting from square one, she and her co-founder Kennedy Odede worked non-stop to establish the Kibera School for Girls in 2009. Their nonprofit, Shining Hope for Communities (SHOFCO), is opening a healthcare clinic there this year.

> "The deck is so stacked against these people that I care about. But I see moments of transformation, and I would do anything to help them." *—Jessica Posner*

I learned about this remarkable 23-year-old graduate of Wesleyan University from Echoing Green, a global nonprofit that awards seed funds to social entrepreneurs working on bold ideas for social change.

I reached Jessica in Kibera working on her various projects and wanted to ask her how she ended up in Kenya launching such groundbreaking programs. And how was she able to start the free girls' school?...

EYE: You're one of the social entrepreneurs that Cheryl Dorsey of Echoing Green mentioned to us. She said, "They bleed for their issues ... they own them." How do you describe your passion to help the people of Kibera?

JESSICA: It was when I was in college at Wesleyan University. While I was there, I studied abroad and worked on a theater project with Kennedy Odede, a young community leader in Kenya. I have a background in theater for social change, which uses theater to tell stories about people's lives.

I found a tremendous need for something to change the way things were. Kennedy and I kept working together and started the first school for girls. It definitely was challenging work and hard. The deck is so stacked against these people that I care about.

But I see moments of transformation, and I would do anything to help them.

We are absolutely changing lives. Look at the girls at our school. Last year they didn't speak; they were shut down. Now, a year later, they speak English, read, write, and do math. They could be kids anywhere. I see great hope and possibility.

EYE: Why did you choose Kenya?

JESSICA: It was fate possibly. I wanted to go abroad and do something very different, so I found a program at the School for International Training. I applied and then found myself in Kenya.

EYE: You've said that Kibera is hell on earth. Describe this hell and what you're trying to do.

JESSICA: Kibera is a hard place to describe. Every day I feel differently. Each day is always good and hard. There is tremendous resilience here. These are incredibly smart people who drew the short straw.

It is absolutely a tough place. No one should have to live in these conditions. There are 10 people in a room 10x10 feet.

Children sleep in cardboard boxes. There is no formal electricity, no running water and no toilets.

Kids are going to the bathroom everywhere. There are no formal schools. It is really lacking all basic infrastructure.

> **I think that I've learned how unfair the world is. Of course there are times when it's really upsetting. It makes me more angry than anything and fuels me to work harder.**

We start from square one and aim to provide basic services. We try to give people skills and the power to prove that anything is possible.

EYE: How different is this experience in Kenya from the way you grew up?

JESSICA: I have never wanted for anything. This is totally opposite to my background. I'm from the middle class in Denver. I had everything. I knew that there was a world very much not like where I lived that was hard for any of us to imagine.

EYE: No white person had ever lived in Kibera before you moved into a slum there when you were 20. Describe your living conditions.

JESSICA: I moved to a 10 x 10 room without running water and with no electricity. What I saw was devastating.

The people had no access to education. It's amazing what people can acclimate to. It saddened me that they had to. I became close to this community. I lived there for two-and-a-half months. I went back to the U.S. that year during the Kenyan political crisis.

EYE: The area where you lived was set on fire after you left. Many people were killed. Yet you went back. Why?

JESSICA: My future husband Kennedy was still there and at risk. I helped him get out of the country. He wanted to go to college. I told him to apply to Wesleyan, and he did and was accepted. I decided to go back the summer before he came, to do a theater project about violence. The people were sad but there was no active violence then.

> It definitely doesn't always go smoothly but that encourages me. I like challenges and things not going perfectly. I look past obstacles.

EYE: Starting the Kibera School for Girls was a true challenge. You had no money and nothing to begin with. How did you get it off the ground?

JESSICA: Kennedy and I talked about it a lot. He wanted to start a school for girls. When he came to

Wesleyan, there was a grant for $10,000 available. I said we should apply, and we got the $10,000.

The school started with 45 girls. We built eight classrooms with a library. Everything cost under $20,000. We ended up fundraising for the rest. We were able to graduate our first class.

The school has electricity but it's been out all week. The education is free but parents have to help out for no pay. They get water from a well 30 minutes away.

EYE: You won VH1's 2010 Do Something Grand Prize Award for being a Top World Changer. That's a $100,000 prize. How did you win this?

JESSICA: I just applied. They selected 15 finalists and flew us all to New York. Then it was down to five and I won. All the money goes to a large-scale purified water project that we're working on.

EYE: How much of a thrill was it to win?

JESSICA: All of a sudden I was in Hollywood getting the award from stars on a live television show. I still wonder if it really happened. It was surreal, a different world and a fantastic experience. The next day I was on a plane back to Kenya and Kibera.

EYE: You call your School for Girls ground-breaking. How so?

JESSICA: It's the first free school for girls. It places emphasis on the value of girls' education in the community. The curriculum was designed just for us by education experts from around the world. It's very hands-on, like the Montessori Schools.

The kids are very involved. They have big challenges. They have to love going to school; they have to be excited.

They are four to nine years old, preschool to second grade. We're hoping to get to a ninth-grade level. We have 67 girls now and add a class every year.

We're working with partners to get them to a high school they don't have to pay for that provides scholarships.

We see such a change in their overall demeanor; there is a nobility there. Every year we take another 15 students. Eventually we hope to have 570 students. Even that many is not enough. There are so many girls that need to be given a chance.

EYE: Will you continue expanding or try to set up schools like this elsewhere?

JESSICA: This school could be a model. We are definitely interested in linking tuition-free schools for girls to community services wherever possible. This community has embraced the idea.

EYE: What have you learned from your efforts to help the people of Kibera?

JESSICA: It's amazing to me what people can do for themselves. I'm so pleased to have gotten to facilitate it.

> When people are given leadership, they can do amazing things. We have people come in every day and say they have an idea. It's very organic.

EYE: What's one thing people can do to help your efforts?

JESSICA: There are a lot of things. It's great for people to know about us. They can sign up for the newsletter, make a donation and read our blog on our website. We're on Facebook. The biggest need is probably money.

EYE: How long will you stay? What more do you hope to accomplish?

JESSICA: It's hard to say how long I'll stay. We're excited to open our new health clinic soon.

People need access to healthcare and to be treated with dignity.

We built the fourteen-room clinic from the ground up. The paint is going on today. It's a primary care facility and also has a women's care program. It's funded by Newman's Own Foundation. It will have a prenatal care, post-natal care, well-baby care and access to family planning.

EYE: What about the women of Kibera?

JESSICA: It's about class in Kenya. In the affluent part they're making progress and there are opportunities. When you live in extreme poverty, it's hard to make progress. All of our girls come to us living on less than one dollar a day.

I think that in ten years there is hope that the value placed on women will be different. I would wish that our girls will see a different future, that they can do whatever they want to and perhaps change their community. One goal is that our girls will be able to lead productive, sustainable lives that make them happy.

EYE: Many thanks, Jessica. And good luck with all your projects. You're making an incredible difference in this community.

First published in October, 2010.

Marsha Wallace

Marsha Wallace on How Dining for Women Wants to Feed the World

By Stacey Gualandi

While meditating in 2002, Marsha Wallace had a vision: "What if every month you meet with your gal pals, you take the money that you would normally spend at a bar or restaurant, and then donate that money to help poverty-stricken women and girls half way around the world?"

> **"I do believe if you ask you will receive. We're best when we're living with purpose..."** —*Marsha Wallace*

Sounds like a simple concept right? Well, that inspired idea became Dining for Women, Marsha's organization that boasts more than 200 chapters in the U.S. and in three countries, and has raised more than $946,000 for 48 charities in developing nations.

I confess cooking is not my thing, but dining out with friends is. I was looking for a fun way to make a difference, so I connected in more ways than one when I spoke to Marsha...

EYE: You've had great success since your first dinner party. How does it feel?

MARSHA: I am grateful. Yes, and surprised, because initially when I had the inspiration for DFW, the inspiration didn't come like "Hey, I want to create a national organization."

> **Being a nurse, a wife, and parent with young kids, and with no background in philanthropy, it would have scared me to death. I wouldn't have started it had I had some grand, huge vision.**

I feel gratitude that the idea resonated so well with people because it never felt that I was trying to pound a square peg into a round hole. It really did take on a life of its own.

EYE: You received more than $30,000 in donations in three consecutive months. You must take time to pat yourself on the back.

MARSHA: I don't feel like I personally did it; the universe has conspired to help me. The things that have happened have been synchronicity, miracle after miracle and coincidence.

It certainly has been one amazing thing after the other that has propelled us along. I've just done the best that I could to keep us on the right track. I am proud of what we've accomplished. It's just that I know that it wasn't all me!

EYE: We both practice TM (transcendental meditation), and it was while meditating you had the idea for Dining for Women. Do you still meditate?

MARSHA: Yes! Since this idea came to me while meditating, I've been afraid to quit! Ha! That was one great inspiration. I don't want to miss anything else!

EYE: You are a nurse by training, but why did you feel that there was still something else you were supposed to do?

MARSHA: I had been seeking for many years. I was restless and at a point in my life where I was really asking the universe to show me what I needed to do. I wanted to find my passion. It was a constant mantra for me. I just felt compelled; I can't explain it.

I do believe if you ask you will receive. We're best when we're living with purpose and when we do whatever brings us joy—that spark to be excited and enthusiastic.

Giving back gives you a sense of purpose. It's different for every person. I think we all have the ability. The vision and enthusiasm come naturally.

EYE: Has DFW been challenging? How difficult has it been to follow through on your vision?

MARSHA: It has been difficult. It's required a lot of work. The vision and enthusiasm come naturally. What have been difficult and challenging are the logistical and operational parts of making it happen.

The right people have come along to help, but it has required time and focus and dedication. During the last few years my family has felt like I have been absent because I've been so focused on DFW. They've felt that I was distracted all the time.

My husband and I went to therapy a couple of times to talk about it. We had many, many conversations about boundaries and priorities, so I don't want to make it sound like it's been a walk in the park.

EYE: Do you have any regrets?

MARSHA: I don't regret anything. I think because I've seen the impact and we have been growing, it's been rewarding and totally worth it. This whole organization is 99% volunteer-run. We hired an executive director so now some of the burden has been lifted. I can breathe a sigh of relief, but it was what was required at the time.

EYE: I think this whole idea is smart and oh, so simple. But I am not a cook. If I didn't have to have a kitchen, I wouldn't! I do, however, enjoy getting together with friends. How hard is it to get started? Would just $200 in the first month be enough?

MARSHA: That is tremendous! Our average donation is right around that amount per chapter. The average monthly donation per person is around $30, give or take. I don't even like to cook.

This idea of DFW wasn't revolving around the food or the cooking so much as it was the communal aspect of getting together with other women.

Some do brunches, wine and cheese, tea and cookies. One Arizona chapter calls themselves "Wining for Women." The format is flexible; it just depends on the collection of people in the group and what they want it to look like.

EYE: With this tough economy, could I get people to join and donate?

MARSHA: It depends on the group and whether you want to invite the public or just let people know in your community, maybe through an article that will draw like-minded people who you might not even know.

We are about to expand into an alternate level of membership through "virtual chapters." And we want to explore Skyping.

But we really want at the core to nurture individual groups of people who do come together and connect face-to-face.

EYE: Can you be charitable and philanthropic but not be wealthy?

MARSHA: Absolutely! That's the whole power of collective giving. If each average donation is only $30 per month and if you think the average family spends $250 a month out, all we're saying is take what you would spend on one meal and donate it.

You don't have to sell all your possessions. It's totally doable. So your $30 can turn into $30,000 because you've added it into this pot from all these other people who share this common goal. That is very powerful.

What will that look like when we're ten times bigger than we are now? What kind of impact can we have? One woman said to me recently, "What is great about this concept is that it is 'the democratization of philanthropy.'"

EYE: The *Huffington Post* declared this the "decade of women-focused philanthropy." Is this true?

MARSHA: Yes. There's a focus on women and girls from the donor side. It's becoming so much better now with the power that women and girls have to change global poverty. It's sort of an idea whose time has come. Author Nicholas Kristof says it's "the moral challenge of our time."

The more I've learned about this, the more I've realized that we were on the right track all these years, even though I didn't know what I was doing. This is not a feminist whim.

> **Studies show it's women and girls who have the power to change the economic state of their communities and countries, and that all leads to a more peaceful world.**

EYE: Is there one story that touched you personally and represents what you are trying to do?

MARSHA: One of our programs is Matrichaya, India. We have donated to them for five years, which is not typical. Our first trip to India was in 2007. One family—a mother, daughter and granddaughter—all benefited from the money DFW donated.

We helped start vocational training and literacy programs from scratch. The mother and daughter got that training and made enough money so that now the granddaughter is getting an education! So that's how the change happens.

EYE: You have said that DFW has a long way to go. What is your goal for the next few years? And beyond?

MARSHA: In a nutshell, I envision having a network of women all over the world who make these contributions, still on a small scale. The idea is that we have this collective giving on an immense scale but still maintain the intimacy of small groups.

Short-term in the U.S., I want us to be a household name. I want there to be more towns where there is a DFW chapter. There is so much room to grow. I want this information about the power of women and girls to be better known.

The education is as important to me as the money that we donate.

EYE: Why not donate here in the U.S. instead?

MARSHA: This is the most asked question I get. There is a greater need internationally. That tells me people are not aware of the desperate situation all over the world. Two hundred dollars can go a long way. That amount could start five businesses alone.

EYE: What is your fondest moment? You've talked about working with The BOMA Fund of Kenya [now called The BOMA Project of Kenya].

MARSHA: I'm proudest when I get to meet face-to-face and hear from our program directors directly. We went to Kenya one year and at a leadership summit in Atlanta, Kathleen Colson, the woman behind The BOMA Fund there, gave a report that examined the money we donated.

BOMA received enough funds to launch 60 businesses of five women each. Dining for Women members changed the lives of 300 women and more than 1,500 children. It was a tangible impact. That's what it's all about.

> **I'm so happy when I hear from new chapter leaders and they say, "I was looking for something like DFW my whole life."**

My goal is simply for anyone to have the same joy and fulfillment as I have. When members feel as empowered in their souls as I do and the average person has fulfilled their dream for making a difference, what more could I ask?

EYE: Thanks so much, Marsha. I'm sold. I want to start a chapter in Los Angeles and can't wait to let you know all about it after our first party!

First published in February, 2011.

Photographer Barbara Massaad at refugee camp,
Bekaa Valley, Lebanon

Photographer-Chef Barbara Massaad Brings Lifesaving Soup to Syrian Refugees

By Pamela Burke

When you see photos of the refugees streaming out of Syria, you wonder how these people can endure the journey to another country, how they can find food and safe shelter for their families. They seem to be facing impossible odds.

If not for humanitarians like Barbara Abdeni Massaad, who is reaching out to these nomads with her *Soup for Syria* project, their struggle to survive would be an even greater challenge.

> "I went to visit the refugee camp, not really knowing what to expect or what one could do to help. But my visit brought me closer to the problem and inspired me to find a way to ease someone's pain."
> —*Barbara Massaad*

We met Barbara through our TWE pal Beth Howard, AKA The Pie Lady and author of *Ms. American Pie*.

Beth had travelled the world promoting cultural tolerance with her one-of-a-kind pies and out-.reach. She met Barbara in Lebanon and told us about Barbara's special *Soup for Syria* cause and cookbook.

When we heard about Barbara's passion to help refugees, we wanted to spread her message on TWE. Thanks, Beth, for the introduction. And now we want to introduce you to photographer-chef Barbara Massaad, who is living in Beirut, Lebanon...

EYE: What got you involved with this humanitarian cause of bringing soup to Syrian refugees?

BARBARA: The idea of the cookbook came before the soup distribution actually. I was in my apartment in Beirut and I was freezing cold. I had put the heater on and still I was so cold. That night I couldn't sleep thinking about refugee families in the Bekaa Valley sleeping in their tents 40 miles away.

How were they able to beat the winter cold? *I shouldn't be complaining*, I thought to myself. *How can they survive?* I was really worried. We heard on television of children dying because of the cold. I couldn't go on with my life and ignore theirs.

During Mass on Sunday, a friend of mine who works at the United Nations told me about a campsite nearby and gave me the contact of a person I could call.

I went to visit the refugee camp, not really knowing what to expect or what one could do to help. But my visit brought me closer to the problem and inspired me to find a way to ease someone's pain. This is when I started taking photos of the refugees and talking to them about food.

EYE: Did you ever think it would turn into this book, *Soup for Syria*?

BARBARA: I am a cookbook writer and photographer so it was natural for me to do that. Weeks later, the idea came about to do a humanitarian cookbook. A good friend of mine called me one day. She was also very concerned about the current situation in the camps, stating that she wanted to make soup for the refugees.

We both work for Slow Food Beirut and decided to go to the farmers' market and give out her homemade soup to refugees in Hamra. This is how the idea of doing a soup cookbook came about.

EYE: Why is providing warm soup so important? Why soup?

BARBARA: Soup is comfort. Soup is home. Soup is nourishing. I have always had a special feeling for soup. When I was a little girl, I would tell my dad soup warms my heart. It's like a security blanket for the body and the soul.

EYE: What do you hope to accomplish with this project?

BARBARA: Awareness that we are all in the same boat. We all have basic needs. Families are suffering; we can't just live our lives and let them live their hell. We can't ignore the pain of others.

EYE: Is this interest in humanitarian issues something that has been your passion for a long time or has it been developing?

BARBARA: I can't just watch people suffer and do nothing. I have empathy and am very sensitive to children's suffering. I am a mother of three children.

EYE: You live in Lebanon, and we read where you are criticized for not helping Lebanese children in the same way you are helping the children of Syria. How do you deal with that criticism?

BARBARA: It hurts a lot, especially when it comes from friends whom I have known forever, and then I discover they don't understand my point of view. They are parents, too, and yet have no empathy for this cause.

EYE: You and your publisher, Michel Moushabeck, were able to attract more than 80 celebrity chefs and cookbook authors to give you recipes. Was that difficult?

BARBARA: Actually, it was not. We had great enthusiasm from almost everyone we approached. We are both very dynamic and worked really hard to make this happen.

EYE: Talk to us about your eye for photography. What do you look for when photographing your subjects? What did you see in the eyes of the people, especially the children?

BARBARA: I am the daughter of a well-known photographer. Photography was always a part of my life; food, too! When someone is sensitive, photography comes easily. I have the ability to put people at ease and succeed to get them to trust me—that is 80% of a photo.

The rest is magic. I am very at ease with children and they are with me, so it's like a

**game we play and they express what they
need to express as I take their photos.**

EYE: Tell us about a favorite soup that you prepare.

BARBARA: I simply love the roasted pumpkin soup
recipe. You all have to try it.

EYE: What have you learned from this experience?

BARBARA: I learned humility. I learned to accept
everyone regardless of any negative stereotype. I
learned that war is never a solution to any problem
and that the ones who pay for war are innocent
victims, mostly women and children.

EYE: Can you describe the resilience of the Syrian
refugees you've met?

BARBARA: The situation is very hard to accept. I
visited the camps yesterday, and instead of being
immune to the situation after two years of visiting
them, it is affecting me more.

A 15-year-old girl had an operation, and because
of the donation of an angel who has empathy, we
were able to help out. I visited her as she was just
coming out of the operation and what I saw was
my own daughter lying on this hospital bed, weak
and confused.

She looked at me. It made me cry. People, there is so much to do, so much pain. There is so much injustice. I repeat again and again: We are all in the same boat, all looking for the same basic needs. No, I can't get used to this situation where families live in terrible conditions year after year.

EYE: Is *Soup for Syria* a model that could be duplicated to help others in similar situations?

BARBARA: Yes, of course. It is basically a way to give comfort to those who suffer by offering food relief, understanding, and a clear message to the world.

EYE: Do you think of yourself as a modern-day crusader for a cause you believe in?

BARBARA: I think of myself as a mother who knows what it is like to have a family and to want to protect that family. In turn, this is what drives me the most—children and families suffering for the injustices of war.

> **I believe that all families all over the world have basic needs, and those needs need to be met no matter what in order to survive and live with some sort of dignity.**

EYE: How did you decide where to give the profits from the book?

BARBARA: It was a joint decision taken by my publisher and me. A contract was drawn out and the most important factor for me was to have the money used for a food fund relief for Syrian refugees.

EYE: What's next for you? Will you continue with this project?

BARBARA: I will continue to collect donations and goods, to buy food and help those who need hospital fees paid. If I can help in any way, I will be doing it. Of course it's not me alone, but all the people who were involved in this project who make it happen. Each one contributed greatly to the success of the book and project.

EYE: Thank you, Barbara. We admire your care and concern for these refugees. Keep up the great work!

First published in October, 2015.

Paola Gianturco

Paola Gianturco Shines the Light on Grandmother Power

By Stacey Gualandi

If you love photographs that take you to new corners of the world to meet fascinating people like we do, you will want to pick up a copy of Paola Gianturco's beautiful book, *Grandmother Power: A Global Phenomenon.* Paola is a renowned photographer who has made a career of documenting women's lives. This time her subjects are more than 100 grandmothers in more than 15 countries.

> **"I was on five continents and everywhere I saw the same thing—energetic, effective grandmothers doing important work."**
> **—*Paola Gianturco***

I was thrilled to talk with Paola about her special journey to capture the spirit and stories of these indomitable activist women...

EYE: Whistler once painted his mother in a very grandmotherly pose in a rocking chair looking very subdued. How do you think Whistler would paint a grandmother now?

PAOLA: I think he would have to paint women going to the gym and running businesses. Half of all the grandmothers in the United States today aren't even 65 yet. They are too young to retire.

Today's grandmother is very different. She is younger than she's ever been. She is roughly between 45 and 64, better educated, very healthy and has a great work experience. Many of them are baby boomers who came of age in the '60s, and they know they can change the world because they already have. There are many effective activist grandmothers.

EYE: So many of your photos are magnificent. They seem to come to life. How long have you been doing this now?

PAOLA: This is a second career for me. I was a businesswoman and not a professional photographer or writer. I worked for 35 years in marketing and corporate communications in the business side of those businesses.

I thought I would take a one-year sabbatical, but I never went back. It was during that

**one year that I began photographing
women and creating books about women.
That was that. And this is book number five.**

EYE: Were you always someone who took pictures and felt comfortable behind a camera?

PAOLA: Yes. My father put a camera in my hands when I was eight years old. I never had a class but I quickly took some when I realized that I was going to be serious about this.

EYE: You must have a natural ability. You have that good eye for that great photograph!

PAOLA: I stood behind many good photographers who worked for the agencies and businesses I worked with, so I had lots of experience behind the camera even though I wasn't doing the actual shooting.

EYE: What feeling comes over you when you take a picture that captures the perfect image? Is that something you think about?

PAOLA: I think very hard about who it is that I am taking the picture of and how well the picture represents the person I have come to know. I do the interviews before I do the photographs so that I have a strong sense of who these women are and what their lives are like before I begin to take the pictures.

EYE: What was your first book, the book you did during your sabbatical?

PAOLA: The first book was *In Her Hands: Crafts-women Changing the World*. It was about women artisans in twelve countries on four continents, all of whom were sending their children to school with the money they earned from making handicrafts and selling them.

EYE: You are not someone who is adverse to travel?

PAOLA: There is a reason I can do this work. As a result of having worked all over the world, literally, I started with one million frequent flyer miles on United Airlines. I could go virtually anywhere for free and stay anywhere.

My husband had two million additional miles, which he gave me because he was excited about the work I was doing. So I was able to do all of these projects relatively inexpensively.

It then makes it possible to donate the other royalties from these books. They are all philanthropic projects giving to organizations that are working on the issues in the books.

EYE: You are literally not making a dime?

PAOLA: No. But I don't have to pay anything to fly or to stay in hotels. I pay for my own meals, but I would have to do that if I were home. Thanks to shooting digitally—it used to be very expensive to buy lots of film and then have to process it—it has really made a difference.

EYE: What was the inspiration for this latest book, *Grandmother Power*?

PAOLA: I was working in Kenya and interviewing women there who were actually part of a women's water project in the rural part of the country. I asked them, as I often do in an informal way, how many children they had.

I was fascinated that they all virtually responded that they had two children and eight adopted or "I have three children and fifteen adopted" or "I have five children and ten adopted."

Suddenly I realized they were really telling me that their children had died from AIDS and they were raising their grandchildren.

EYE: How did that strike you?

PAOLA: I was struck by the sadness that represented.

I got tears in my eyes. What do you say to give each other comfort?

These women were not strong enough to carry water on their heads, nor were they able enough to work or earn money. They were very poor. Suddenly they had more than a household of very young children all over again, just when they thought they were at the time when they could relax.

EYE: Of course these women would take these children in, right?

PAOLA: Children always run to their grandmothers after the funeral. They and their grandmothers are still grieving. It's just a catastrophe. So many grandmothers are like that all over the continent of Africa.

This was in 2006. When I came back, I thought that the future of this continent rests in the hands of these grandmothers!

EYE: So, that is what you wanted to bring out in your book?

PAOLA: I wanted to bring these women's voices to people's attention. I was on five continents and everywhere I saw the same thing—energetic, effective grandmothers doing important work.

EYE: What do all these women share?

PAOLA: The attributes that were threaded through all the stories are really values and behaviors that I think are very important to teach young people. They include generosity, collaboration, patience, perseverance and resilience.

EYE: Who were a couple of the 120 outstanding women you met on this five-year journey?

PAOLA: There were some Indian grandmothers who went to school at the Barefoot College in Rajasthan, India. After six months they learned to become solar engineers. They returned to their villages and installed solar panels on the roofs of their huts.

Everything changed. Midwives could see to deliver babies at night. Children no longer got black lung disease from studying by kerosene lanterns. They can charge cell phones, which means they can do electronic banking. They have refrigerators that keep their food bacteria-free.

By now there are ten thousand hospitals in India that have been solar-electrified by grandmothers. The United Nations got wind of this huge success and began sending grandmothers from all over the global south to study with these same grandmothers who went back to teach at Barefoot College.

Now there are at least 35,000 households in 24 countries in all over the developing world that have been electrified by grandmothers.

EYE: Now, I understand, there are grannies at Israeli checkpoints?

PAOLA: Yes. Israeli-Jewish grandmothers are monitoring checkpoints to quell and stop human rights abuse against the Palestinians. People are often trapped in the checkpoints for hours and hours without explanation. Sometimes women give birth there; many miscarry and die.

People have been denied medical access and trapped in the checkpoint. There have been 50 or 60 who have died out of some 991 denied medical access. There are catastrophic results in terms of human rights abuses. The Jewish-Israeli grandmothers concluded that this was untenable.

They began going two-by-two to the checkpoints and monitoring soldiers, which was very courageous and controversial because some of them had soldiers in their own families. They issued reports daily to the Knesset, the media, journalists and internet. They have gained respect.

EYE: Amazing! Activist grannies are all over the world! It reminds me of the Raging Grannies.

PAOLA: There are 60 gaggles of Raging Grannies in five countries. In fact, I photographed the San Francisco Raging Grannies Action League, who do great work.

They even play songs to raise awareness of issues they think will either benefit or work to the detriment of their grandchildren. They are terrific and fun.

EYE: Are you trying to unite these groups?

PAOLA: It really surprised me how many grandmother groups there are that we may not be aware of. I am also hoping that people will start their own—join, network with or support other groups.

EYE: Is there one image or photo that represents who you are as a documentary photographer?

PAOLA: I suppose the cover of the book. It's the photograph of a Senegalese grandmother. She and I were dancing with all the grandmothers in her grandmother group. They danced me to the car.

I photographed her through the window of the car, just as we were about to leave. You just never know when you are going to take a photograph that is that iconic.

It just makes me smile every time I see it. She has so much joy and so much energy that really embodied what I discovered everywhere.

EYE: Can you tell me where the proceeds for this book are going?

PAOLA: The publisher is paying 100% of my author royalties to the Stephen Lewis Foundation in Toronto who grants funds to groups of grandmothers in 15 African countries who are raising children orphaned by AIDS.

Everyone who buys a copy of the book is contributing importantly to their work.

EYE: Thank you for bringing this issue of grandmother power to the forefront. I'm sure many people will be thanking you.

PAOLA: I hope many people will get involved. It takes grandmothers and grandothers to provide hope and possibility for our world. I have presented 55 slide lectures throughout the U.S. and Canada to let people know about the power of grandmothers.

I know of two groups inspired by the project that are working on health issues: one, a group of U.S. volunteer nurses who are teaching grandmothers about health and nutrition in rural Uganda and another educating the public about the need for vaccinations.

EYE: You have the ball rolling, Paola! Thank you so much for taking the time to talk.

First published in July, 2015.

Part II:
Improving Children's Lives

"Let us remember: One book, one pen, one child, and one teacher can change the world."

—*Malala Yousafzai*, Nobel Peace Prize Winner

Maggie Doyne and some of the children at
Kopila Valley Children's Home in Nepal

Maggie Doyne Changes the Lives of Nepali Orphans in the Blink of an Eye

By Patricia Caso

Maggie Doyne is thrilled any time one of her forty kids, 3 to 16 years old, calls her "Mom!" Taking a gap year after high school, she wound up as Founder and Director of Kopila Valley Children's Home and School in Surkhet, Nepal. Maggie is realizing her dream to create a loving home, school and community for orphans and abused children.

> **"The hopelessness I witnessed was monumental. I found this horror was reality for 80 million kids worldwide. How did I not know about this? I had to do something and I had to do it now."** —*Maggie Doyne*

Wise beyond her 27 years, Maggie has amazing passion and courage. I was fascinated by this young woman and wanted to find out how she was able to house and educate so many children in such a poverty-stricken community.

In the midst of a busy schedule of meetings on a trip to the U.S., I caught up with her by phone....

EYE: At 18, you delayed going to college and were volunteering at a Nepalese refugee camp in India. At what point did you know you weren't going back home to New Jersey?

MAGGIE: I met a Nepalese refugee, Sunita, in the Indian camp. She offered to show me where she came from, and I was curious to find out why so many Nepalese children, who were civil war refugees, ended up in India. I had no idea what I was getting into. I ended up busing for two-and-a-half days and hiking with her for two more days to a remote part of the war-torn Himalayas.

> **I saw poverty on a scale I had never seen or imagined before. There was a whole community of desperately poor kids, mostly young girls, breaking rocks into gravel by the riverbed.**

They hauled bags on their backs to make a dollar for food. Every day Heema, who was six or seven years old and carrying heavy pounds of rocks on her back, would engage me with the Nepalese, "Hi!"

Why wasn't she at least in school? I wondered. The answer was that it cost too much—$5.00! Other child porters had no family, no home. What have we done as a human family that people should live like this? It was the first time I ever felt ashamed to be human.

The hopelessness I witnessed was monumental. I found this horror was reality for 80 million kids worldwide. How did I not know about this? I had to do something and I had to do it now.

EYE: Where did you start?

MAGGIE: I saw the future and worked backwards. I wanted to create it. I called my parents to get my $5,000 from my babysitting money to buy land and build a home. I wanted these kids to have a safe home, health care and education.

Many don't make it past five years old. I was 19 when I launched my project. Nisha was the first child I adopted. Now I have 40 kids living in Kopila Valley Home and over 300 enrolled in school.

Working primarily with Surkhet community, then with donations, grants and volunteers from around the world, I was able to build this beautiful slice of hope.

EYE: What do you mean by "working the future backwards"?

MAGGIE: If we want to have a healthy, blossoming, peaceful world, then we need healthy, blossoming well-taken-care-of children with good childhoods. That was clear. I saw kids having a childhood like I had, with enough food to eat, a family, a home base and a really good education.

That was my goal. I wanted to flip these kids' worlds around with love, through having a home and a family. Everything I started to create was based on that.

> **I have found you have to trust your inner voice, follow your heart. If you are doing work you love, everything else tends to fall into place.**

EYE: What is the meaning behind the name Kopila?

MAGGIE: It is the Nepali word for "bud." The local community organization also helped choose the word because we thought it represented what children are all about. They resemble a bud. If a bud gets everything it needs, it will bloom magnificently.

EYE: You deferred college to find your "inner self." What have you found?

MAGGIE: Before I was 18, I thought I had to follow the same old beaten track that everyone else was going down. Until I stepped out of that bubble of fear that *I have to be this* or *I have to be that way*, I didn't realize that the world opens up to you.

EYE: How does your youth work in your favor?

MAGGIE: I left home when I was 17. I was 18 when I put the wheels in motion, and 19 when I was in Nepal. I was definitely a young person. The mindset is that you can do anything, that nothing stands in your way. I think young people are visionaries. They don't worry about things.

EYE: Did you worry about staying in touch with people back home? You seem to have found social media very helpful.

MAGGIE: Social media is the reason I was able to share the message with the world. For the first three or four years I was living in Nepal full-time in a very remote region in the Himalayas. The only way to communicate with family and friends was through a blog.

Slowly it became a Facebook page, then we went on Twitter, and Instagram followed. Anyone can now instantly see what's going on day to day on the ground. That connection is so important. People feel that *Nepal is not that far away,* or that *the life of a child there is not that different from life with my own child here.*

If you look at the goodness in social media, it is about humanity. We all have similar

> joys and sorrows. I want to paint a picture
> of what it means to be a child in the devel-
> oping world, what it looks like.

EYE: What is the meaning and purpose of your BlinkNow Foundation?

MAGGIE: I believe that in the blink of an eye we can all make a difference. BlinkNow Foundation is a vehicle to share my ideas with other young people. It's a grassroots organization to empower young people to become pioneers in developing their own solutions to world poverty.

The site targets underdeveloped war-torn countries where extreme poverty, high rates of illiteracy, disease, child labor and unstable governments exist. People can also find ways to volunteer, donate to Kopila Valley efforts and find out what is going on with the kids and me.

I named the organization BlinkNow because, for me, it was an instant decision to stay in Surkhet with all these children. No doubt in my mind. How could I ever go back?

> My life was just changed forever. In my
> case, I picked up, moved and started rais-
> ing money in the blink of an eye. I think
> we all have to live our lives that way.

EYE: What are you focused on at Kopila Valley now?

MAGGIE: We are concentrating on organic growth and approaching problems at their source. We built Kopila Valley Home to keep the children safe and housed. Then we needed to give these kids a school so they could have a quality education. Education is a catalyst for change. We also established a nutritious lunch program to address hunger.

A medical clinic was created to address the infections and diarrhea that they were battling at home, and it became a community outreach clinic. We launched a women's center because too many issues involved violence against women, their equality and so on. It has expanded to include a store in town.

We are also trying very hard to make Kopila Valley a locally sustained project from what we eat, to the medicine we use, to what we wear, to the building materials, everything.

EYE: What concerns do you have about girls in school?

MAGGIE: If it were up to the Nepali cultural and religious tradition, they would give preference to their sons. In 2004, girl enrollment was 26% and in 2012 it went up to 72%. If you talk to a woman in Nepal over the age of 30, it is very unlikely that she has any form of education at all, or that she can hold a pencil and write her name. Additionally, girls face challenges with trafficking and child labor.

So we wanted to swing the pendulum in a different direction. I've been a big follower of the Girl Effect, which is all about including girls in education, health and economic investment.

Women and girls tend to stay within the community, whereas men tend to leave. Women reinvest a lot of their income back into their family, passing it on to their own children.

EYE: Speaking of children, what are the toughest and most rewarding parts of parenting all these children?

MAGGIE: The toughest is the fear that something bad is going to happen to them. Are they going to make friends? Are they going to do well in school? I worry about their happiness and their health. At the end of the day, when you're totally tired and all you want to do is sleep but somebody is having a temper tantrum, it's trying to keep cool and patient.

There are 300 students at the Kopila Valley Children's School. Juggling and managing time is another concern so that they get my best self, my most quality self. I want them to see me as being totally present with them. The most rewarding thing is definitely watching each of them grow into their own person, with their own thoughts, their own ideas, their own successes.

At some point you just look at them say, "They are really a person." When they first come to you, they are little beings who are suffering and struggling. Then they have their favorite music, they read books, they make jokes. They hug you and tell you that they love you.

EYE: How do you manage to keep balanced with all this work?

MAGGIE: I really had to learn how to disconnect. My home life, my work life and everything that I care about are all wrapped up together. I read. I try to meditate. I try to get into yoga, but I am a terrible yogi. Every now and then I take in a good movie. I stay in touch with friends and run.

EYE: Maggie, your vision is transformative. I encourage readers to check out BlinkNow to learn even more. Thank you for your time, and please accept our sincere wishes for continued growth and success to you and your Kopila Valley family!

First published in December, 2013.

Elissa and Marzia from Afghanistan leaving hospital
after her operation

Elissa Montanti Stands by Wounded Children Around the World

By Pamela Burke

We saw a fascinating piece on CBS' *60 Minutes* about Elissa Montanti, an amazing woman who brings children with missing limbs from all over the world to the U.S. to be rehabilitated. Her endless determination to help young people survive and prosper is remarkable. Once you hear Elissa's story, you don't forget it.

> **"You are giving children their dignity, their youth and new friends from a different corner of the world."**   —*Elissa Montanti*

We found Elissa on Staten Island in New York and were delighted we could talk to her about her inspirational memoir *I'll Stand By You—One Woman's Mission to Heal the Children of the World.*

She told us about starting the nonprofit Global Medical Relief Fund from her closet on Long Island with one child, Kenan, who had lost one arm and both legs in a land mine accident. More than 150 children had followed him to Elissa's "Dare to Dream" House. This interview will give you a taste of her drive and determination to make a difference...

EYE: You have an amazing story, Elissa. My heart goes out to you and all the children you have been involved with. You have accomplished what few could by launching this Global Medical Relief Fund, which you ran out of a former walk-in closet. What propelled you to start this fund?

ELISSA: The need I saw in the suffering children. How could I not try to do something?

EYE: You had a job as a medical assistant and gave it up to start your organization. Were you scared that you might not succeed? That was quite a leap you took.

ELISSA: Yes, but my desire and determination to do so were stronger than my fear of not succeeding.

EYE: Have you accomplished more than you ever thought you would?

ELISSA: Actually it was my goal to do as much as I possibly could. Yes, I have accomplished a lot but there is much more to do.

EYE: I read that your slogan is "Never Say Never." How do you keep such a positive attitude?

ELISSA: Because that's what keeps you focused. If you allow negativity to dominate your desire then you will build barriers with a big blinking sign saying, "No entrance."

By saying "Never Say Never," the road before you is always wide open with various options and opportunities.

EYE: You've spent over 14 years using most of your own money to bring children who need new limbs and new lives to this country. How do you keep going financially?

ELISSA: On a wing and a prayer and lots of peanut butter sandwiches!

EYE: You say you run on a prayer, begging and borrowing money. How do you persuade people to get involved? Do they ever turn you down?

ELISSA: I show them a child's picture and letter of plea. How can they say no? However, I did receive a "no" once from a hospital whose policy was not to treat foreign children. It's their loss for not making a difference in that child's life.

EYE: I heard you say you get hate mail for bringing children in from some countries. Does this bother you?

ELISSA: It used to. But now I say a prayer for those who send me those types of notes.

EYE: The story of the plight of Waad, the young boy on *60 Minutes*, was amazing. His continuing recovery is a miracle to behold and the result of your efforts and those of all of the people involved. Do you stay emotionally involved with these children forever? Did you think Waad would ever be able to play soccer as he did on the piece?

ELISSA: Yes, I knew he would. It never gets old to me to see them walking, running, reaching for a glass or writing. I stay in touch with almost all my kids, especially the young children who will return to the U.S. for follow-up treatments until they are twenty-one.

EYE: You say that you are more than an organization…that the children you are involved with become ambassadors to the world. How important is that to you?

ELISSA: Very! It's about the healing and the coming together of all ethnic backgrounds and living under one roof. They all look out for one another, speaking different languages but communicating through love.

It's about the kids going back as little ambassadors and showing the more positive face of America. And so much more.

You are giving children their dignity, their youth and new friends from a different corner of the world.

EYE: I read that you say you cry all the time. How could you not? Experiencing what you do must be heart-wrenching. How do you keep going?

ELISSA: I do cry a lot, and I can't prevent it. I've tried but the lump in my throat hurts too much to hold back my tears. Knowing that I am making a difference keeps me going.

EYE: You brought three children back from Haiti after the earthquake. There was and is such a need there. How do you decide whom to help?

ELISSA: It isn't easy but you try to prioritize as much as possible. You ask yourself who has the worst injuries and who would benefit the most. Of course there is the approval of doctors and hospitals, that they can in fact help.

EYE: Your job seems overwhelming. There are so many children who need help. Do you wish you could do more?

ELISSA: Absolutely! I want to do more, and I will strive to do as much as I can in my lifetime.

EYE: What is your dream for your organization? You moved in to your "Dare to Dream" home, where you can house more children. That is quite an accomplishment!

ELISSA: It is a milestone, and I am filled with pride. My dream is to help as many children as I possibly can.

EYE: How can people help? You talk about small actions being very important.

ELISSA: In my book's introduction, there is a story about "The Starfish Thrower." It goes something like this...

A man is walking along the beach and notices a woman going back and forth, again and again, between the water and the sand.

As he gets closer, he stops and laughs. This crazy woman is actually picking up the starfish stranded on the beach, one by one, and tossing them back into the ocean.

"Lady, look there are thousands of miles of beach and God only knows how many of those little creatures," he says, shaking his head. "One person can't possibly make much of a difference in saving them."

The woman stoops down to pick up a glistening purplish starfish, dusts it off, and gently casts it back into the waves, then turns to the man and smiles. "It sure made a difference for that one!" The starfish story has become a metaphor for my charity.

I am that crazy woman, and the injured children I bring to the United States for a new limb and a new smile are like those starfish.

People can help by visiting our website. They can also buy my memoir, *I'll Stand By You*, which tells the story of how and why I found my charity, my struggle through depression and finding that by putting these children back together, I was healing my own shattered self.

Portions of book sales will benefit the Global Medical Relief Fund.

EYE: What's next for you?

ELISSA: To grow, but never so much that I don't know whom I am helping. These children are not numbers; rather, they are part of my global family, whom I truly love.

EYE: Thank you so much, Elissa. We will stay in touch and want to learn more about you and your most selfless undertaking.

First published in September, 2012.

Jenny Bowen

Jenny Bowen's "Half the Sky" Saves Chinese Orphans

By Stacey Gualandi

All it took for Jenny Bowen to step up was a *New York Times* photo of a malnourished little girl in a Chinese orphanage. That's when she decided to save lives thousands of miles away.

> "It doesn't matter if it's Chinese orphans or what it is. If you see something wrong in the world that needs fixing, you can do something." —*Jenny Bowen*

This former screenwriter is the founder of Half the Sky Foundation, an organization dedicated to improving the lives of Chinese orphans and the way they are cared for. To find out how she single-handedly changed a government's thinking on child welfare, you can read her book, *Wish You Happy Forever: What Chinese Orphans Taught Me About Moving Mountains*.

I'm honored to have had the opportunity to talk with Jenny, who spoke with me from Washington D.C...

EYE: Before this part of your life with Half the Sky, had you ever been to China?

JENNY: My first and only trip to China before Half the Sky was to adopt our daughter Maya.

EYE: You were a screenwriter, a mother; you had two grown children. What was going on with your life before you found Maya?

JENNY: I would say my life was pretty comfortable, although maybe not particularly meaningful. I was an independent filmmaker and screenwriter for hire in Los Angeles. My husband is a cinematographer.

> **Our nest was empty. We had no reason to think we were going to build a family beyond that. Then we saw the photograph in the *Times* of the little girl who was starving to death.**

EYE: Do you remember that first time you saw that picture and what went through your mind?

JENNY: Oh, sure. I think I'd heard about the preference for males in certain parts of the world. But I had no idea that little girls in China were being abandoned simply because they were little girls. The article talked about the really terrible conditions in the orphanages and the fact that many children were not surviving.

Even though we had never considered adopting, we felt like we had to do something. The typical middle-class response is to send money. But, whom do you send money to in this instance? My husband said—I didn't say it—that we could bring one child home. And that's what we did.

EYE: There are many different crises around the world. Why did this one speak to you?

JENNY: Until I wrote this book, I really had no idea why. I felt absolutely that this was the right thing to do at the time. When we went to China to adopt Maya, we felt we were saving a life. Instead, it transformed my life. Maya came to us with pretty much all the effects of institutionalization, everything that is wrong with institutionalization.

She was not quite two years old. She was malnourished, had parasites and amoebic dysentery. She couldn't walk or talk. She was emotionally shut down. She was vacant. We saw what almost two years of neglect had done to a child. We didn't know what to do, even though we were experienced parents.

> I did what parents instinctively do; I
> brought her home and loved her up. I was
> in her face every waking moment. Her first
> words were part of the dialogue from my
> movie. I didn't care what she was saying.
> I was just so glad to hear her talking.

Then, about a year later, we were having a party at our house. I looked out the kitchen window and there was our daughter romping around in our garden, singing and calling out to her friends, so happy and full of life and joy. She looked like a child who had been adored from the moment she was born. And, that was just in a year. I thought *That was so easy. Why don't we just do that for all the kids we can't bring home?*

EYE: You probably asked yourself, *How can I not do something?*

JENNY: Exactly. That's how I felt. Honestly, from that moment I did not look back. I walked away from everything that had been and I did this thing. I knew what I had to do.

EYE: Is this a rare situation or was this commonplace in the Chinese welfare system in the late '90s and early 2000s?

JENNY: At that time, it was the standard. China was really caught between the collision of the one-child policy and the traditional preference for boy children. By the late '90s—we adopted Maya in '97—the orphanages were just full of healthy baby girls.

It was a crisis. Children who were abandoned and living in orphanages were low on the priority list. At least they were getting fed; they had shelter and some of them were surviving. Those were some of the lucky ones.

EYE: You've really had to educate the orphanages on ways to improve the situation. What kind of impact have you had?

JENNY: The impact has been incredible. Now I consider the Chinese government our partner, our true partner, because they have completely and proudly adopted our approach to transforming children's lives.

We are now working on a six-year initiative with the government to train every child welfare worker in the country in our approach. The impact is going to go way beyond orphanages.

It's going to be helping street children, migrant workers' children, children taken into child slavery and trafficking and all these horrible social issues.

These children will now slowly be able to benefit from the simple, basic premise that all children need to love and be loved. Without that, they cannot thrive.

EYE: There's one photo in your book that shows these kids tied into their potty chairs.

JENNY: It's not because the caregivers don't love children. Nothing like that at all. It's because they were overwhelmed. And there was no training, no standard for hiring caregivers. People were just assigned to those jobs, whether or not they had experience with children. They tied them to keep them in order so they would have some control.

There would be one caregiver and 30 babies. If you're a mom, you know what one baby can do to your day! So these caregivers were not bad people; they were not trained people. They were ignorant people. They were not given any resources beyond the basics.

EYE: So, the Half the Sky concept and organization filled that void.

JENNY: Yes, it certainly did, although I can't pretend it was immediately recognized as the solution. It was a long haul.

EYE: Now what do you mean by "half the sky?"

JENNY: It's an old Chinese saying that women hold up half the sky. It's attributed to Chairman Mao, even though many say it was said long before him.

When we brought our daughter home, 95% of the children living in the government orphanages were little girls. We wanted to help them hold up their half of the sky.

EYE: Did you have any idea how to create your own organization?

JENNY: No. I was utterly unqualified. I didn't speak a word of Chinese. I'd only been to China once before and that was to adopt. I had never thought about starting a nonprofit organization, an NGO. I had never dealt with a government bureaucrat.

All I knew about child development was what mothers know. I had no qualifications except that I was a filmmaker and a screenwriter and I knew what to do with a blank piece of paper.

I knew what to do with nothing. I could imagine a world that didn't exist and I

could imagine how to make that world happen.

I could imagine a happy ending and how to get there. So, it's really like I'm making a movie and I've been in production for the last 16 years.

EYE: You also have Anya, now. How have these children changed your life?

JENNY: My two girls, who are now 18 and 16, are living proof that nurturing care can transform a child's life. They are doing great and I am just a lucky mom, just an ordinary lucky mom.

EYE: What kind of resistance did you get when you stepped foot into China and said, "This is what I want to do." Were they receptive to you?

JENNY: No. But, they knew something had to happen. There had been a lot of international criticism just before I got there. There was a documentary called *The Dying Rooms* that tried to expose the dark secrets in Chinese orphanages.

Then there was a Human Rights Watch report that was actually the reason that I saw that photograph in the *New York Times*. It was attached to an article called "Death by Default—A Policy of Fatal Neglect in China's Orphanages."

They were under so much international criticism. By the time I got there, the doors were closed to foreigners.

EYE: So, how did you get in?

JENNY: As a filmmaker, you always find a way. I just talked to everybody. I finally found somebody who found a half-Chinese, half-German advertising executive who had a contract with a Chinese NGO. He made an introduction that got me the introduction that got me the introduction that got me the introduction that got me in the door. That's very much the way China works; it's probably the way a lot of places work.

Half the Sky has directly impacted about 100,000 children and probably more. We have indirectly impacted millions.

EYE: What can we do? What do you tell people who want to help, who want to try something like this?

JENNY: Look at me. I am ordinary. I have no qualifications to do what I have done. It doesn't matter if it's Chinese orphans or what it is, if you see something wrong in the world that needs fixing, you can do something. You can. You really can. It's true.

I am living proof that it is true. Ordinary people can make a difference.

EYE: I want to thank you, Jenny, for talking with me today. Continued success to you and Half the Sky Foundation.

First published in September, 2014.

Estella Pyfrom

Estella Pyfrom's Brilliant Bus Closes the Digital Divide

By Patricia Caso

Estella Pyfrom, a 2013 CNN Hero, is simply "Gadget Lady" to the children she serves on Estella's Brilliant Bus. This second-oldest daughter of seven children grew up in the segregated South. She was part of a migrant worker family that traveled from Florida to New York and back during the summer months.

> **"I had to think of a way to get technology out to the underserved neighborhoods. I knew I was going to need a vehicle of some kind...so my option was a bus."**
> —*Estella Pyfrom*

Four years ago Estella retired after 50 years as a teacher and guidance counselor in Palm Beach County, Florida. When we spoke, I found there was no "tired" in retired for her. Estella could not turn her back on the kids who she knew were falling behind because they had no access to a computer. Her brilliant solution?

Buy a bus, outfit it with computers and roll it into underserved neighborhoods to beat the digital divide between the haves and the have-nots. Thus, the Brilliant Bus...

EYE: What exactly is the "digital divide?"

ESTELLA: We are in the age of technology, digital literacy. Kids who do not have access to a computer and that technology due to poverty and other issues are left behind. Digital technology is critical to education, just like reading and writing are crucial to connectivity, to modern learning style. It is a must for kids to learn this, to be a part of an even playing field.

EYE: How on earth did you decide to use a bus as an answer to the digital divide?

ESTELLA: I had to think of a way to get technology out to the underserved neighborhoods. I knew I was going to need a vehicle of some kind. The van I had would not be big enough.

> **I thought of a semi-truck, one of those 18-wheelers, but I couldn't drive that. So my option was a bus. I learned to drive a bus as a teenager.**

EYE: It seems that an undertaking like this would require a large monetary investment. How much has this cost you personally?

ESTELLA: All the funding came from personal retirement money, some investments and side jobs I had. I've put in more than a million dollars of my personal funds, not all at one time.

The bus, 17 computer stations, infrastructure, the internet, etc. were purchased with my own funds.

EYE: What is your prime mission?

ESTELLA: Many of the children in the underserved neighborhoods cannot get out to get the services they need. So if I can bring the services to them, I think we have a match.

Not only am I taking technology to them, but the technology is in sync with what the curriculum is in the institutional system.

EYE: What kind of staff do you have?

ESTELLA: I have no paid staff. I have very qualified people helping me, who have been school administrators, guidance counselors, teachers and other professionals. Many come from across the state, like web designers. These people say to me,

"This is what I can do. What do you want me to do? I want to help you."

EYE: How do you decide where the bus goes?

ESTELLA: I get emails and referrals now. But I started by going to community health fairs, shelters, schools and community centers. After evaluating kids' needs, I schedule them. I also have a home-bound program to reach the neighborhoods I am not currently serving.

Thanks to a partnership with companies like Comcast, we help families fill out an application so they can get the internet at home. Then, Comcast will arrange an opportunity to get a computer in their home so we can do the reading, writing, math and social studies.

> **I am proud to say that we reach out with technology help, not only with the bus, but also through this homebound program.**

EYE: How many kids have you engaged so far?

ESTELLA: We have reached out to more than 31,000 children over a three-and-a-half year period. The youngest is a group of three-year-olds. Our oldest is 81! We have no age limit in learning or working on computer skills.

EYE: How do you know if the students are progressing?

ESTELLA: Through software I can monitor all the kids' progress. We try to teach the older ones to be independent, working on activities on their own at home. We show them where they started, where they are now and how to keep going until they reach 90% proficiency in their grade level. The younger ones have four to five people monitoring their progress.

> We have not had any discipline problems on the Brilliant Bus yet. Kids understand what we expect from them and they know what to expect from us.

EYE: I understand the Bus does more than roll into neighborhoods, bridging the digital divide.

ESTELLA: Yes, the Brilliant Bus project is actually a movement. Under the Brilliant Bus umbrella, we work with those who feed the hungry and refer for health services, private clinics, doctors, etc. We were asked to go to a homeless village to provide tutoring for some kids ages 5–21.

We also extended an invitation to adults with at least one child, who needed to do a job search or find places to stay. We always look at what we can do for the whole situation and collaborate with partners when we can.

EYE: Were you always a take-charge type of kid in your family?

ESTELLA: I was not always a take-charge type. At age six, because our parents worked, we all had responsibilities. There were some things I could do better because I was a little daring. The responsibility was mine whether I wanted it or not.

> I did what I had to do, which is a bit different than taking charge. Little did I know that I would have a job where I would take charge of things later on.

Yet, I'd rather not try to do something by myself. I would rather join in and get things done using the team approach.

EYE: How important was education in your family?

ESTELLA: Although my father only went through third grade and my mother only went through fourth, they believed in education. They were very smart people. Failure was not an option. They never talked about failure.

They always talked about accepting challenges and doing whatever it took to make things happen. My parents taught us how to share, be responsible and work to overcome challenges.

Whatever your dreams are or whatever your mission is, keep working at it until you accomplish it.

EYE: How did you end up using education to help underserved neighborhoods?

ESTELLA: When I was growing up I never thought about being a teacher. I was very aware that none of my neighborhood families had very much. We shared a lot, helped each other and looked out for each other. It was a way of life.

After traveling up to New York and back with the neighborhood families harvesting produce, we returned and lived in the same neighborhood with these families. Once I finished high school and college I wanted to come back and help my neighborhood. I understood the needs of those communities.

EYE: How did you overcome the educational divide growing up with your circumstances?

ESTELLA: The attitude about migrants when I was growing up was that we would never catch up. You were always going to be behind and you would never graduate from high school. Well, the attitude my parents had about education was that you do what you have to do.

Sure, you have to leave school before it ends for the summer to do harvesting work. You'll also be late coming back. But you have only one option, to make the grades.

> School will already be in session when you return from your work. Yes, you will be behind, but the only option you have is to catch up.

EYE: Do you pass on a similar philosophy to the kids you work with?

ESTELLA: We pass it on. We encourage them not to dwell on all of the negative things. Take what you have and make the best of it. If you program yourself to say *I cannot and will not fail*, then you will continue to work on overcoming the challenges that you have.

EYE: Do you ever sleep?

ESTELLA: I average about four hours of sleep. If I get sleepy, I can always just take a nap. Way back when I was raising my children, I trained myself to work late hours so I could give my kids and husband quality time. Early rising and going to bed late is, you know, the early bird...

EYE: What about the future of Estella's Brilliant Bus?

ESTELLA: I am very optimistic. People from all over the country want to be a part of our team. We want the movement to be in every community in the U.S.

People who have reached out to me from around the world are convinced the project model can be replicated anywhere for communities that are underserved in education, health services, etc. It can be customized.

EYE: You are a CNN Hero. Do you see yourself as a hero?

ESTELLA: No, I do not. I asked my husband, "What's the big deal about all of that fuss?" He told me that I am one of the ordinary people who is making a difference and helping to change the world. No matter how I look at it, I am a CNN Hero.

He also said I am doing things other people are not doing, and I'm not expecting anything in return. That is extraordinary. I just feel that this is what I do. This is what I am accustomed to doing. This is what I know how to do.

EYE: You are definitely a hero, role model and angel to many. Thank you for taking precious time to speak with TWE. Continued success to you as Estella's Brilliant Bus moves to delete the digital divide and so much more.

First published in May, 2014.

Scarlett Lewis

"Nurturing Healing Love" Guides Scarlett Lewis' Life Mission

By Stacey Gualandi

In her book, *Nurturing Healing Love,* Scarlett Lewis writes about her very personal journey following the tragic death of her six-year-old son Jesse at the Sandy Hook Elementary School mass shooting in Newtown, Connecticut. Scarlett gave her book that title because those were the last three words Jesse wrote on his chalkboard before he was killed on December 14, 2012.

> **"It was such a message of comfort that he left for his family and friends. I also knew that it was a message of inspiration for the world."** —*Scarlett Lewis*

Writing about what happened at Sandy Hook began as a way to cope, but for Scarlett it soon became a journey of forgiveness and hope. I was fortunate to talk with Scarlett on *The Women's Eye Radio Show* when her book was released. Here is an excerpt from that interview...

EYE: This book is a great exercise in how to cope

when something absolutely horrific happens. Are you glad you actually wrote it?

SCARLETT: The book has been an incredible, amazing, healing journey for me.

EYE: What prompted the title?

SCARLETT: I was living at my mom's house for about a month after the tragedy. I couldn't imagine coming back to our little, snug farmhouse in Sandy Hook and not having vibrant Jesse, whose energy filled every corner of the room.

On one of our sojourns home when I was getting Jesse's clothes for his funeral—this unimaginable thing I had to do at this time—I came across this message on the kitchen chalkboard. It clearly said, although it was phonetically spelled, "nurturing," "healing," "love."

I knew that was not in his vernacular and that it was a message from his spirit because I just don't think his six-year-old cognitive brain would have thought of those words and put them all together.

It was such a message of comfort that he left for his family and friends. I also knew that it was a message of inspiration for the world. Because of the very public way this tragedy happened, the whole world reached out in the most miraculous show of compassion.

I say that because I was the recipient of that. I feel a responsibility to spread that compassion, along with Jesse's message of "nurturing healing love." It is my purpose in life now. I'm very blessed to have it.

EYE: Where would Jesse, at six years old, have come up with the words "nurturing healing love"?

SCARLETT: I know. It's funny. People ask, "Do you walk around saying, 'nurturing healing love?'" I didn't. I was actually the only single parent of the parents who had children die. I have a full-time job. We had the usual arguments at home, rushing around for breakfast and dinner, and weekends filled with fun.

It didn't come from me. And I know it didn't come from his dad, so the only other possible place it could have come from was a spiritual knowing that he didn't have much time left. With all the other messages that are in the book, I believe that was the case. I do believe there was a shift in consciousness on December 14th.

> **That event changed people in a way that some can't describe—some do, unfortunately, know what this is like—but I believe people**

are on a different path now. It is a path of nurturing healing love. People are choosing love. It's been a beautiful thing to see. It's been very healing for me.

EYE: My dad died on December 14th. It's always difficult knowing that day is coming. How do you deal with the anniversary on such a huge scale, a world scale?

SCARLETT: I did not realize what a big deal the anniversary would be. I think back, and I go, "Wow, on this day last year I was with Jesse." On the last Thanksgiving weekend before the shooting, Jesse was urging me to get a tree. He was my decorations guy. Thank goodness, I did.

He wanted a train. I got a train for him. He got one night to play with the train, thank goodness. After the tragedy happened, I just wanted to get away; I didn't want to be in Sandy Hook. I wanted to be on a beach somewhere just having a lot of fun. That was Jesse's message to his brother, JT, "Have a lot of fun!"

But I had this angst. And my friend said, "What's in your heart to do?" My heart was willing to stay and face it and spread the message of "nurturing healing love." There's a kind of resilience that there's a craving for. And I wanted to share it.

EYE: In your book you say this could be a life sentence of sorrow. Do you think that is true?

SCARLETT: I think it absolutely can be. I think you have to remember you can't control some of the things that happen to you, regardless of the choices that you make. You can always control how you react to situations that happen.

> **The amazing thing is that it's a choice. The choice in handling tragedy is also just that. I knew I wanted to survive.**

I remember blatantly making the decision in my mom's kitchen. Adam killed Jesse but he did not kill JT and he did not kill me. I am going to be the best mother I can be. I am going to survive well. That's my mantra.

EYE: You said a prayer every day from the moment he was born because you had this weird feeling that he might be taken away from you some day. There's the picture he drew of a little boy with angel wings and then there is an evil man standing behind him. Do you think in some way that he knew, or he was psychic in some way?

SCARLETT: I do not think it was psychic. We all have a spiritual awareness but we are all so busy, so distracted. We don't access it. When we slow down, we have it. I think I had glimpses of it when I would say the Jesse prayer, "Dear Jesus, he's a gift. Please don't take him from me."

I am not saying I was wondering if he was going to die early. Not at all. I just didn't question it; I just said that prayer. I don't think Jesse, when he wrote "nurturing healing love" and drew the angel and the bad man, was cognitively aware that something was going to happen.

> **But I do think that spiritually he knew, and I believe that of course he had a purpose on earth and I believe he carried it out, and he carried it out very bravely.**

It very well might have been saving those children. I am very proud of him. I only hope that I can carry out my mission as bravely as he did.

EYE: You mention your son's bravery. Your son was yelling, "People go!" and saving other children by being there, standing and letting them run out of the classroom as the shooter continued. Hearing that, there is a comfort, but can you forgive something like that? You write that forgiveness is like cutting a cord to pain. Can you do that?

SCARLETT: I have. I think forgiveness is this hugely overlooked quality and value that is a must-have for a meaningful and happy life. There are all sorts of transgressions we have to forgive. For me, it's interesting because I talk about forgiveness and "nurturing healing love" with everyone from kindergartners to prisoners.

I was talking to an outreach group at one point when a boy raised his hand and asked, "What is forgiveness?" I said it is cutting the cord to pain; it's not condoning what somebody did, but it is freeing yourself to move forward.

His next question was, "How long did it take for you to forgive the guy who killed your son?" I think when we think about forgiveness, we think it is like a snap decision that we are going to decide to do, like waking up one morning and deciding I am going to forgive Adam Lanza and that's it.

EYE: How does it happen?

SCARLETT: It is probably a process that I am going to go through for the rest of my life. I forgive him every day and sometimes I have to forgive him a hundred times a day. Sometimes I don't make that choice to do it.

When I don't, I feel that anger settling on me like a black, dark, heavy apron; it doesn't feel good.

It's not good for me; it's not good for JT. It's not good for the people around me. It's certainly not good for my purpose in life, which is "nurturing healing love."

EYE: How do you handle the angry moments?

SCARLETT: I take a step back and I take a deep breath and I choose to forgive. As soon as I say that, I'm free. It is such an important part of the equation with healing and joy, which is feeling gratitude regardless of your situation.

> **Believe it or not, through the process of grieving for Jesse, I had to forgive myself for things that I felt I should have done, or didn't do.**

EYE: How did you decide what to do to stop this tragedy from happening again?

SCARLETT: I thought a way to stop it would be to go into schools, to talk with teachers and parents and develop lessons to let kids know they have control of their thoughts. I want to let them know that those 60,000 thoughts that you have in your head every day, the same ones you had last year or five years ago, are not you. They are not who you are.

So, going into schools and teaching about gratitude, speaking about forgiveness, teaching about compassion is what I do.

Compassion is not just empathy; there is an action component where you ease someone else's suffering and teach about character and values.

EYE: Do you think you have changed from the person you were before this happened?

SCARLETT: I certainly like the person that I am today a lot better. Would I give all the changes back to have Jesse back? In two seconds. That's not going to happen so I definitely see this incredible personal growth that is happening in me.

I am sorry it took the loss of my precious son to really get me to wake up and understand how important being of service to others really is; that is really the key to happiness. I have dedicated my life to that now.

That's how I'm surviving and having happy moments. Gratitude, forgiveness and compassion with action under the umbrella of service for others—these are all choosing love.

EYE: Do you think Jesse is proud of his mommy?

SCARLETT: I do. I feel very connected to him in spreading his chalkboard message. There is no way that I could have published a book in eight months, and had Wayne Dyer write the forward, so I know he is pulling strings for me there.

I feel his spirit fingertips on my back saying, "C'mon Mom, let's go. Let's spread the message. That's what we're doing now." I feel very much like it's teamwork with him. For that I am so grateful. I feel his presence every day through my work and I am very grateful.

Incredibly, people from all over the world have emailed me through the website and said, "I am reading the book and feel Jesse's presence. Something like this has never happened to me." I love that. It's his light all over. I know he wants to help everyone heal.

EYE: I wish I'd had the honor of meeting your son. I am so glad to be able to share the message. I sure will practice what you preach.

First published in December, 2015.

Part III:
Empowering Women and Girls

"When we do the best we can, we never know
what miracle is wrought in our life,
or in the life of another."

—*Helen Keller,*
Humanitarian and Social Activist

Holly Gordon

Holly Gordon on Empowering Girls to Transform the World

By Patricia Caso

Breaking the cycle of worldwide poverty is a monumental endeavor. Enter Holly Gordon, the architect behind Girl Rising, a movement to educate adolescent girls around the world aiming to alter their unacceptable course of inequality.

> **"When we start to value girls for their minds, all over the world, we will be honoring their greatest asset. Girl Rising is really about raising the value of the girl."**
> **—*Holly Gordon***

Holly is also Executive Producer of the gutsy, inspiring film *Girl Rising*, which is at the heart of the movement. The movie tells the stories of nine girls in nine developing countries and depicts how education can be transformative.

I was already affected by Pakistani Malala Yousafzai's remarkable story and also girls' rights to education there, and wanted to find out more about this innovative movement. I grabbed a few minutes with

Holly, a lifelong journalist, to learn more about directing an international strategy for mandating equality in education....

EYE: Why was Girl Rising initiated?

HOLLY: We created Girl Rising because it seemed insane to underestimate the extraordinary ripple effect this one intervention—girls' education—would have on so many global problems. It's complicated getting girls to school, keeping girls in school and making sure they learn something.

The biggest drop off for girls is when they hit puberty. So our challenge is to keep girls in school past age 12. If you are going to focus on something, this is a good one to focus on.

EYE: Can educated girls facilitate global solutions?

HOLLY: An 11-year-old at a screening I went to gave me a great answer. She said, "If you don't educate girls then there probably won't be the scientist that is going to solve the difficult health problems." When you aren't educating half the population, you have half the likelihood of having the mental capacity that those human beings bring to solving problems in a community.

We know that a mother will not eat until her kids have eaten and to have mothers with higher level skills, you will have children who are happier, healthier, safer and have a better shot at life.

In most of the world women become the center of the household. They make decisions about healthcare, and statistically, save more, investing their savings into their families at a higher rate than boys. A woman with education also earns more money. That means she returns more to the community because she can spend more.

EYE: Is there a common barrier for girls getting an education in developing countries?

HOLLY: It's different in each case. There are many complexities. Some of it has to do with culture, like child marriage or poverty. Sometimes it comes down to the teachers or poor quality infrastructures.

Threats of sexual violence may keep a girl from going to school due to worry that girls will be attacked on their way. It has a lot to do with puberty. At that point they are fair game for all sorts of predators. It has a lot to do with the value of the girl.

She is most often valued for her labor or her body, not for her mind. When we start to value girls for their minds, all over the world, we will be honoring their greatest asset. Girl Rising is really about raising the value of the girl.

EYE: What goals do you have to achieve this?

HOLLY: The first goal is to change minds by passing the message on through our film, social media, boardrooms, even dinners. Next, changing lives by partnering with pros who have proven track records of educating girls. And finally, changing policy by inspiring leaders to influence governments.

EYE: How does one build a movement to make girls' education viable everywhere?

HOLLY: First, we had to create a network of partners, all of whom shared the same values we share. Educating girls can transform societies.

> We set up several nonprofit partners all around the world who know what it is like to bring girls' education to some of the most difficult places in the world. Then we created partnerships with corporations, the private sector.

Intel is a terrific partner. We also reached out to some of the global A-list actresses in Hollywood and beyond to lend their voices to the film. This garnered attention, made it "hip."

The second part is the content itself. If Richard Robbins, the director, hadn't made such a powerful, persuasive, beautiful, touching, moving film as *Girl Rising* is, we would not have what we have today. The power of the storytelling is really at the heart of the movement.

EYE: Why not make a direct fundraising film?

HOLLY: Our film addresses change as well as fundraising. *Girl Rising* is designed to inspire long-term change. That doesn't mean a simple "give now." You have to inspire people to be part of the change.

It's only an army of changemakers that is going to make change happen. We created an uplifting film showing the hope, the valor of these girls and their courage and determination to succeed.

> **Its message is that if only there were an enabling environment for them. If only they were allowed to live to their fullest potential, they would be changemakers; they would be the revolution.**

There would be change that would be good for everyone. Your responsibility as an audience member is to try to change the rules around these girls' lives. It's a much bigger ask than just giving some money.

But we also want you to create a new event that spreads the word, creates new awareness. Then you are part of the movement, not just writing a check and forgetting.

EYE: What is the defining moment in the film?

HOLLY: I have lots of favorite moments and they change each time I watch the film. I find the Egyptian chapter very moving. The way it is shot, so intimately; the truth and the imagination are very compelling. I also love the moment that Suma, from Nepal, realizes that she is a slave. According to Nepali law, slavery is illegal. Without education, she would not have understood her rights.

EYE: What has Malala Yousafzai, the Pakistani girl shot by the Taliban simply because she was a symbol for girls' education, meant to your movement?

HOLLY: Malala was shot in the middle of filming. It was shocking! My colleague, Tom Yellin, pointed out that it's a stark reminder that what we were doing was timely and important.

It's that dissonance between something incredibly tragic happening, but you know there are going to be ramifications that there will be something good for the world. It pushed girls' education to the top of the global agenda for some time. So that's a good thing, but at what cost?

When Malala spoke publicly at the U.N. for the first time since the shooting, I was moved to tears when it became clear that she not only had all her faculties, but also had a steel resolve and a forgiving heart.

Those two things are what great leaders, iconic leaders, are made of: steel resolve and giving hearts. Malala is definitely a symbol of the movement and she is also a 16-year-old girl. She's funny, humble, and she has handled pressure. Her pressure is to be who she is which is to be an advocate for girls' education. She was that before she was shot.

EYE: Has social action always motivated you?

HOLLY: This project was driven by something actually far more mundane—the story. Of course, I am passionate about girls' education. I am a woman who treasured my education, and it was supported, emphasized, by my own mother.

For me, journalistically, there are fewer opportunities for really important stories to get the attention they need. The film was in progress before I joined the team, and yet of all the projects, this one was identified as the opportunity to change the world.

> **It was global domination for the most important story of our time. That is what I was driven by. And I was driven as a journalist.**

I was motivated by the challenge of not knowing if they could make a good movie about the subject. If they did, then we needed to come up with something so powerful and innovative that would go way beyond one night of television on a network station. We needed it to be in every magazine, in movie theaters and talked about everywhere.

EYE: Bottom line...what do you see the film and the movement enabling?

HOLLY: I'm talking about the film as a catalyst for reform. The film enables the local conversation. I just went to Nigeria because a community organizer there, Michael, arranged a screening in Nigeria with hundreds of nonprofit leaders and school children.

Even though there is not a Nigerian chapter in this film, it allowed for a conversation about early marriage and the rights for the girl-child in Nigeria. That's what followed the screening! That's the way it happens, one community after another.

EYE: Are your efforts sustainable?

HOLLY: We think of ourselves as the hub of a movement. It's sustained by the community leaders who step up and say, "I'm going to bring this to my community." Out of the 100 people at the screening, there will be two or three other leaders who bring it to their communities.

That can be a campus, a company or a neighborhood. They pass it on. Social media has been very important in getting the word out. We try to be a catalyst for leadership and provide tools for the process, so leaders continue and sustain the movement on their own. It will run out of steam when the film stops being powerful or when everyone in the world has seen it.

EYE: Can you point to any tangible progress as a result of Girl Rising?

HOLLY: Two million dollars was raised for girls' education programs around the world. The film has been broadcast in over 120 countries through CNN International. In one month 2,000 events were held around the world by local organizers. There were more than five billion impressions in terms of global media for attention to girls' education.

EYE: Your plan for equality in global education is indeed more than optimistic! May your "revolution" continue taking hold for permanent change! Thank you, Holly Gordon, for your time and insights!

First published in October, 2013.

Gulalai Ismail in Nowshera, Pakistan

Peacebuilder Gulalai Ismail Fights for Girls' Rights in Pakistan

By Farzana Ali

Intro by Pamela Burke

As we know from previous reports from TWE contributor Farzana Ali, northwestern Pakistan is a region rife with religious extremism and violent activity, particularly against women. One brave peacemaker, Gulalai Ismail, decided to face these dangerous forces when she was 16 years old, and has found ways to empower girls by setting up Aware Girls with her sister, Saba.

> **"Being a girl in a culture that discriminated against girls in every aspect of their life created this urge in me to speak for equality."**
> **—*Gulalai Ismail***

Farzana, Bureau Chief for Aaj TV in Peshawar, Pakistan, interviewed this remarkable changemaker exclusively for TWE recently about her continuing efforts to improve the lives of girls and children who are living in a culture of intolerance and given few choices...

EYE: Why did you decide to found Aware Girls? What was your motivation?

GULALAI: I grew up in a culture where women are respected no more than men's property—where girls are taught to have only the dream of getting married and are brought up in a way that makes them a perfect wife and daughter-in-law.

Women are dehumanized in the name of "Honor, Respect, and Culture." They are subjugated to men. The relation of men to women is more like master and slave, so men think they have every right to exploit and oppress women.

Being a girl, I think no one can easily accept it. Everyone wants a life of their own but girls are not given the choices.

EYE: What was it like for you growing up?

GULALAI: I was fortunate to have a father who was determined to educate his daughters. He was a teacher and a human rights activist.

My father brought us storybooks that were about equality and also newsletters that had research about the human rights situation in Pakistan.

He was a human rights activist, so I was able to meet women who were very strong, inspirational and who were leading the women's rights movement of Pakistan.

There were few well-known women in politics, but I believe it's possible to build communities where women can take leadership roles and can make decisions about their own lives.

Being a girl in a culture that discriminated against girls in every aspect of their life created this urge in me to speak for equality. I started by writing poetry and making drawings on the issue of discrimination against girls. My family was thrilled to see me speaking up against gender discrimination.

EYE: When did you start to become involved in issues involving girls?

GULALAI: My father mentored me and linked me to opportunities for strengthening my leadership skills and knowledge. I became part of Child Rights Advocate Forum, which was an opportunity for me to reach out to other girls.

I soon realized that many girls have internalized the discriminatory norms and values and find little space to raise their voices. It gave me the motivation to create a platform for young women and girls so they can raise their voices for their rights.

As soon as I started high school I, my sister, and other friends decided to establish Aware Girls.

EYE: Tell us about the problem of extremism and young people in Pakistan.

GULALAI: Our youth are victims of indoctrination and terrorism. They need unbiased, unprejudiced education that can give them the skills to think rationally, rather than fall for propaganda. Our education system and political propaganda have indoctrinated youth and made them the victim of terrorist groups.

EYE: How do you protect girls from violence, especially after the attack on Malala Yousafzai?

GULALAI: In our culture women are victims of both patriarchy and extremism. Research shows that young women under the age of 18 are the ones who mostly become victims of domestic abuse. Violence against women in Pakistan varies from early and forced marriages, and domestic abuse, to cultural practices and honor killing.

We at Aware Girls are working to prevent women from becoming victims of violence by advocating with the state—both provincial and federal—to set in place systems that protect the right of women to live with dignity and be free from violence.

We strongly advocate for laws against sexual harassment, domestic abuse and to protect the reproductive health rights of women.

EYE: What are some of the ways you reach out to provide assistance to women and girls?

GULALAI: We are running the Marastyal Helpline, which provides information, counseling and referral services to shelter homes and legal aid to women who are victims of gender-based violence.

We also engage girls in initiatives such as digital storytelling for addressing violence against women. The purpose is to highlight the plight of Pakistani women using social and digital media innovatively.

EYE: What is the secret to turning youth toward productive activities and away from extremism?

GULALAI: We don't see young people as "terrorists"; we see them as victims of prejudice and indoctrination. The secret is to understand where the hate, bigotry and violence come from.

Young people who have access to information—

who have an understanding of the progressive face of religion, who are aware how religion is used by terrorists and some political groups to grab power—are less vulnerable to the militant groups.

EYE: How have you been able to get young people access to positive information?

GULALAI: Through our peace-building work, which we started five years back with the name "Youth Peace Network," we have developed 12 groups of young peace activists. We have provided them training in skills for countering extremism and building peace in their communities.

More than 300 young people from different parts of the northwest of Pakistan, such as FATA, Swat, Dir, Buner, Shangla, Chitral, Peshawar, Swabi and Charsadda, are members of the network. Through education on nonviolence, pluralism and peace they counter extremism and promote peace.

> **These young people are our partners in promoting nonviolence and peace in their communities and preventing young people from joining militant groups.**

EYE: The *Daily Beast* reports that five million people have been displaced by violence in Pakistan, with 33,000 people killed since 2003. What is it going to take to turn the country away from this senseless brutality?

GULALAI: We need a multi-winged strategy to address violent extremism in Pakistan. As a youth activist, I believe peace is not possible without engaging young people as equal partners in peacebuilding. Instead of seeing young people as problems and trouble creators, we have to see them as part of the solution.

The government and civil society have to engage young people in the peace initiatives as peace-builders. We have to teach love in schools instead of bigotry and hate.

EYE: How do you have the courage to drive to the dangerous northern part of the country through checkpoints in the middle of the night to meet with young people?

GULALAI: My family and I have been under surveillance and have been attacked for the peace and human rights work I am doing. We have been accused of being western puppets and CIA agents. All these attacks and accusations speak of the impact of my work.

It means the work I am doing is having an impact on young people and therefore there are groups who feel threatened and try to create hurdles for me. It gives me strength. I get my motivation and my hope in the stories of young people who learn nonviolence through our peace work.

We commit never to engage with any violent group who imposes their ideology and who vows to promote intolerance in Pakistan. There are thousands of stories in our work that give me strength and courage. I seek my motivation in these positive actions of young people for a better Pakistan.

I will continue my work for peace and prosperity, no matter how risky it is, because I believe change is not possible without us speaking up and taking action.

EYE: How do you persuade mothers to get involved? Are many afraid?

GULALAI: Aware Girls mostly works with young women in the Khyber Pakhtunkhwa Province. They are mothers, daughters, sisters and wives, but they are human beings too. Through our work we have learned that they are brave and knowledgeable.

They have the passion to work for their communities and to make them peaceful. Every year hundreds of girls join our programs with the hope to contribute meaningfully to their communities by acting as agents of change.

EYE: You visited Washington, D.C., last year and met with President Obama and members of the administration. How did that help you?

GULALAI: In 2013 I received the Democracy Award in the U.S. Congress by the National Endowment for Democracy, and was then invited by the White House to attend a meeting with President Obama on the shrinking spaces for civil society around the globe.

I also got the opportunity to meet Samantha Power, Ambassador from the United States to the United Nations. She was supportive of the civil society. Later in the year I was recognized as one of the 100 Leading Global Thinkers by *Foreign Policy* magazine of the U.S.

These meetings have helped me to convey my messages of peace, shared responsibility and accountability to the global community, which are equally important to local struggles for peace and human rights.

EYE: Do you see change happening within the youth of Pakistan to form a more peaceful country?

GULALAI: Change is a slow process. I am very glad

to see that they are now politically more active. They are concerned about what's happening in their communities and they want to play their roles in making the situation better. We receive applications from hundreds of youths who want to join our peace and human rights programs.

It shows the interest of young people in playing their role as agents of change.

EYE: What are your goals for the future?

GULALAI: For now, nonviolence and tolerance are the most needed in Pakistan. These are our indicators to prosperity. Educated—unbiased education rather than indoctrination in the name of education —and empowered young people, especially young women, can change the fate of Pakistan.

EYE: Thank you, Gulalai. You are an amazing role model for women all over the world!

First published in September, 2014.

Jerrie Ueberle

Jerrie Ueberle's Academy for the Future of Women Aims to Change the World

By Patricia Caso

Jerrie Ueberle is a no-nonsense leader to be reckoned with. Leadership is the very quality she intends to instill in young women worldwide through her World Academy for the Future of Women. She wants them, globally, to share equally in advancing the planet and to lead fulfilling lives of their choosing.

> "When we bring women into the Academy, they discover they have a voice, a choice, a path to discover their purpose and their passion and the path to success."
> —*Jerrie Ueberle*

I wanted to know more about the woman who has taken on such a monumental task. I caught up with this seven-day-a-week social entrepreneur by phone in Phoenix, Arizona and learned more about what makes this vision a necessity...

EYE: Why did you decide to initiate the World

Academy for the Future of Women? That sounds like a huge goal.

JERRIE: I had attended the United Nation's Women's Forum in 1995 in China and in 2000. Conversations from that forum developed the United Nations Millennium Development Goals. I was absolutely thrilled with the possibilities of addressing basic human issues like poverty, hunger and education.

Then when I revisited it many years later, I noticed that the 15-year plan had not nearly been achieved, and some of the issues were even greater than when they were announced as a Millennium Goal in the year 2000. The only thing I could identify as missing in achieving the goals was leadership, specifically for women.

On May 3, 2009, in Henan Province, China, at SIAS International University, I announced the World Academy for the Future of Women. The Academy opened for the academic year in September, 2009.

EYE: Did your day job also tip you off that women needed attention?

JERRIE: Global Interactions, my nonprofit, is my main job but World Academy takes up the majority of my time. Since 1984, we had connected teachers with teachers, doctors with doctors, surgeons with surgeons and people from emergency management, etc.

Yet, out of those successful connections and notable progress, I wasn't seeing a lot of women in these partnerships.

EYE: What was it about China that made you want to start your Academy there?

JERRIE: I'd previously worked and given conferences in China with Global Interactions. I was very aware that 100 million people live in Henan province and most of them are agrarian. Many of them are certainly living at poverty level; people make less than a dollar a day.

The women and men at SIAS University in the Academy represent that population. So everything we do for them, they can do for their village. This part of China seemed to be the perfect place to proactively teach leadership, making change a reality.

EYE: What myths exist about young women in China?

JERRIE: Myths like village women are shy and probably not well educated, that they are not motivated and are destined to repeat the cycle of poverty. When we bring women into the Academy, they discover they have a voice, a choice, and a path to discover their purpose and their passion and the path to success.

As a result, we just need to get out of their way. They are inspired about what they can do for themselves and for others. I think the "and for others"—service—has been the most significant attribute of the Academy.

> There is so much to do on this planet that is totally fulfilling and is recognizable as the result of the effort you put into it.

EYE: Would you say that leadership is not just about moving toward financial success?

JERRIE: We're not about simply leadership training for corporate executives. We're more interested in changing leadership to look at basic human values. One of my board members said we should hire "bored" executives to get the job done!

Those would be executives who are not fulfilled with their corporate leadership roles and are much more passionate about having humanity succeed.

EYE: What is the potential for students involved in the Academy?

JERRIE: We are looking at what's possible for women who saw no possibility for themselves and men who saw no possibility other than life repeating itself in jobs that are not personally fulfilling.

There is so much to do on this planet that is totally fulfilling and is recognizable as the result of the effort you put into it. It's work, but it's not monotony, and it's not sacrificing your soul. It's enriching. I want our students to understand their productive capacities.

EYE: How did you make WAFW a reality?

JERRIE: I came home from China after making my announcement and was struck with the fact that I had no idea what I was taking on or how I was going to do it. So, I just put it out on the internet and people started to respond.

Men and women leaders have taken the challenge to learn how to devise a leadership curriculum. They become facilitators. Many cannot afford the airfare to China and the five weeks that the program takes, but they've let this idea touch them.

They've raised money; they've talked to their employers and said that this is something they need to do with time off.

EYE: What qualifies one to be a facilitator?

JERRIE: Facilitators are skilled in leadership training and generous with their time and resources. Facilitators must be flexible and must have had a broken heart and bruised knees. Wisdom and experience go a long way.

A successful applicant also has the sense that she could do more with those talents to be fulfilled. Facilitators are responsible for creating an environment for these students who don't even know they can dream.

EYE: What can students participating in WAFW expect?

JERRIE: Their academic curriculum is first and foremost. The Academy is extra, and students must spend 8 to 10 hours a week in the Academy programs and activities in addition to their academic curriculum.

Also, students do not get university credit for their Academy work. Leadership is not about credit;

leadership is about service. This is rigorous. So they really are there committed to providing a service, to developing.

EYE: I also understand each student must commit to one Millennium Goal for her tenure with you.

JERRIE: We produced a three-day event within the United Nations program to end poverty in September, 2010. We've continued to ask the students to make noise, take action and stand up.

On the first day each Academy student signs a commitment card selecting which Millennium Goal they will stand for.

EYE: Is going back to improve their villages a goal?

JERRIE: Going back to the village is not the goal. I care wherever they go that their village and that the issues related to the Millennium Goals are in their hearts and minds. So, if she is a ballerina, she dances because she knows women in the village have not had opportunities and have not had an education.

In whatever positions they hold, I want them to be sensitive to a much larger population than that of their corporation or their customers or clients. That sensitivity should make them responsive in social networking, social media, and community campaigns for HIV Aids, alleviating poverty or giving students opportunities for education.

It is a part of their fiber as a woman or man that this awareness is ongoing. It is part of any leader's spirit.

> One of the things the kids say at the end of a year is that they are braver and have more courage to take risks. They have to learn the courage to put themselves out there.

EYE: In addition to risk-taking, do Chinese students from these rural areas face other barriers?

JERRIE: Yes. The ability to see what needs to be done. These students grew up in villages that look a certain way. Environmental insanity like debris, polluted water and garbage all over the place is taken for granted.

And they've come to see that as their village; rather than it being offensive, it's home. When I go to the villages, we sleep three in a bed, no latrine; it's a hole crawling with maggots, very sparse, no flowers, no grass. It's not pretty.

So they don't see the possibility of things being any

different. They often don't see their family or friends being different. That's just the way it is. So lacking vision, or being really able to say, "I can do this!" is a huge area for us to address with them.

EYE: How did you know your vision for these students was working?

JERRIE: I knew it when a student stood up, talked about her dream to own a bakery, went home on holiday and asked a local baker if she could learn how to bake cakes. Another young woman, who participated in the Academy and barely spoke English, ended up being a translator for a glass factory in her village area, traveling to Finland, the Czech Republic, Germany and Poland as an interpreter.

EYE: Has this journey with the Academy changed you?

JERRIE: I think I am not as serious as I used to be. I am a more joyful person.

EYE: What do you see for the Academies for the Future of Women and Men?

JERRIE: Certainly we have challenges to find funding for all the international requests to establish Academies in other countries and continue with training facilitators. Yet, when all is said and done, I believe the Academy is unstoppable in weaving together hearts and minds.

EYE: Thank you, Jerrie, for sharing your insights and details of your amazing work. Continued success to you and especially to your Academy students!

First published in November, 2013.

Maman Marie Nzoli

Maman Marie Nzoli,
An Unsung Congolese Hero

By Amy Ernst

I arrived in North Kivu, Democratic Republic of Congo, in April 2010, from Chicago. I was introduced to Maman Marie Nzoli through a local Catholic priest who knew of my desire to help survivors of sexual violence. I work alongside COPERMA, the NGO that Maman founded in 1983, raising funds, identifying new survivors of rape, and helping arrange medical and psychosocial support for all victims of the war.

> **"We want so badly for the violence against women to stop. We have to hope, otherwise there is no point in continuing to help."**
> —*Maman Marie Nzoli*

The work I do is miniscule compared to that of Maman Marie and the loyal COPERMA team. She has established 12 centers that have assisted thousands of men, women, and children over the years around Butembo.

Even though they often aren't paid, Maman Marie and her team work tirelessly, never turning down anyone with need nor hesitating to go into a dangerous situation. They've subsisted mostly on selling potatoes cultivated by beneficiaries of COPERMA.

She's an unsung hero and an endless inspiration to me. Here is what she told me recently in her small concrete office in Butembo, Democratic Republic of Congo...

EYE: Maman, what was your childhood like here in Congo?

MAMAN: I was the fourth child of my family. I wasn't a child who was given the privilege of a good life. My parents were teachers, but I lived in a rural environment.

> **In our family, we couldn't eat without working. I started to wash my clothes by hand when I was seven years old.**

EYE: How did you make money as a child?

MAMAN: In secondary school, I started making beignets—fried dough balls—to make a living. I also prepared peanuts to bring to the school and sell to the other kids. For the rest of the school fees, I collected coffee beans during vacations to buy the notebooks and materials.

That's how I finished secondary school. In order to get a better education, I went to live in Musienene—a small village in Eastern Congo just outside the city of Butembo—with another family, where there was much famine.

EYE: Was there peace when you were growing up?

MAMAN: When I was a child, there wasn't complete peace. There was robbing when the military found you on the road. They would take your money if you had any. If you had anything in your hands, they would take it.

But there wasn't the sexual violence like now. That was rare, and there wasn't a lot of killing.

There were still a lot of young girls who became pregnant too soon.

EYE: How did you avoid that happening to you?

MAMAN: I avoided it because I had a lot of fiancés. I told myself *If I sleep with them, the fiancés won't respect me anymore.* There were so many men who asked me to marry them. But I chose one person.

EYE: When did you get married?

MAMAN: It was because of the influence of others that I married at the age of 20. It was in style. I married the first man to actually present the dowry. I went to Bukavu, capital city of South Kivu, for higher studies.

We had three children. My husband was a soldier in the FARDC, the governmental army. He went to Kinshasa, the capital, and I didn't hear from him again.

EYE: Why did you decide to found COPERMA and work to help others?

MAMAN: When I came back from Bukavu after my studies, I went to Masareka. We were living with country women. We reflected on their problems and organized a group of 18 women.

With those 18 women, we decided to make an NGO (non-governmental organization) because we couldn't find fields to cultivate, and without that we couldn't make a living. We saw that we all had the same problem and that we should work together to figure out how to increase and facilitate production.

When the war began in 1997, the problems increased. It wasn't just making a living anymore but remaining safe. Women and girls were being raped and boys were being taken into armed groups.

COPERMA began working with those urgent problems while still trying to help with cultivation and living.

EYE: Do you think the needs are growing or diminishing in North Kivu?

MAMAN: The need is growing because the number of problems is growing as well as the gravity of each one. There are little girls who are only 15 and 16 years old, and they are pregnant.

With famine, even though this country is very fertile for cultivation, many people are still starving. Young girls with children and no husbands will struggle greatly to feed themselves and their children.

EYE: What about the problem of sexual violence?

MAMAN: It is increasing. Now it's not only the rebels but also governmental soldiers and many times the civilians who rape. It is becoming a part of the culture that it is okay.

If a rapist is caught, he can be freed immediately by paying the police or the jail. There was a girl of seven who was raped by a man in a prominent family. He was arrested and a member of that family paid some money, and now he is free. The girl's family is devastated and angry but what can they do?

> There's also the problem of having to hide what you've been through so you won't be ostracized, which prevents men, women, and girls from getting help for medical problems.

EYE: How do you help the rape victims, especially the young ones?

MAMAN: We help them first by bringing them to a center that can provide them with free medical treatment and some basic psychosocial treatment. We must bring them somewhere that can provide the PEP (Post-Exposure Prophylaxis) Kits.

After that, we do follow-up in the centers to help them emotionally overcome the trauma so they can live their lives without being terrified all the time. We help also with the primary and secondary schooling since most of these girls won't have access to education and can't pay the school fees.

To help them develop economically, we have programs in the centers that teach sewing, breadmaking and soapmaking. We try to help them with physical health, emotional health and vocational training.

The help we give to adult women versus children only changes in terms of how urgent the cases are. If a girl is twelve years old and is raped, we try to give her more assistance and make her a priority because she is much more vulnerable than a woman who is grown.

EYE: How do you maintain your strength after the traumatic experience in 2005 when 18 children in the COPERMA center were killed while hiding?

MAMAN: We guard strength because those things are the affairs of war. After instances like that, I often stayed in bed for many days. When the children were killed in the center during a confrontation in Luotu, those who survived were hidden and closed in the center for three days with the children who were killed. Many of them became sick, and the shooting was very serious.

I couldn't find my strength after those 18 children were killed. I was so angry. I was hoping the government would help the children after that but they didn't do anything.

**We have no government in Congo. I knew
that if I didn't find the strength nobody
would help the children.**

EYE: There was another terrifying event when you
were rescuing girls who had been raped on the road
by rebels.

MAMAN: When we went to Luotu in 2006, there
was sexual violence in the road in front of us. They
were raping the girls amidst the shooting in the
road. It was the different groups of Mai-Mai rebels
and governmental forces, and they were all mixed
and all of them were starting to rape the girls.

**We ran into the car because of the violence.
When the shooting and raping stopped, we
ran out of the car to help some of the girls.
We brought some back to the car and took
them to the hospital.**

The women were all bleeding from their wounds,
and they were crying. They were so upset. When
it happened, I thought about it a lot. After that
incident I was also traumatized. I didn't feel
good, and I couldn't understand why this is always
happening to us.

EYE: What helps you overcome those frightening
and seemingly hopeless thoughts?

MAMAN: When I find myself with others in the psychosocial training sessions, for example, I find strength. When you experience incidents like these, you mustn't stay alone or you won't be able to continue working. The thoughts of what you've seen will play too many times in your mind.

You will become hopeless. You would want to just stay in bed always. We're trying to explain to others that all of the problems can pass. We listen to music or we recount what happened so we can feel normal about it.

EYE: Do you experience fear?

MAMAN: I often am afraid, but I say to myself that if I stay in that fear, I can become sick. Fear is a sickness, and it can bring on physical sickness, so one must try to face all of the fear that's there.

I'm afraid when I'm around guns, which are everywhere here. The military causes fear in my heart always, because of one day when they made us take off our clothes on the road to Goma. Everyone in the bus was made to strip and they stole our clothes. We drove off with everyone in the bus naked.

When we arrived, I had hidden some small money and I bought clothes for everyone to cover them-

175

selves. But truly I was afraid. I am always afraid of the military.

They're animals; they forget the characteristics of men and take on the characteristics of animals. Even on the side of the road they rape. They are not men.

EYE: What's your biggest wish for COPERMA?

MAMAN: Ah! I would like it if COPERMA could succeed at helping the girl-mothers and the victims of sexual violence and also help them psychologically. Someone who is traumatized can't work; they have trouble continuing to breathe and live.

> I want to effectively help the rural populations because they're often forgotten. Where are the structures that can help to give the people in the villages the hope to live?

We can identify the cases and encourage the victims, but we don't have the means to help everyone.

EYE: Is there hope that this violence will stop? The *American Journal of Public Health* reported in May, 2011, that 48 women in Congo are raped every hour, 1,100 each day, and 400,000 per year.

MAMAN: Yes, I hope it's going to stop because

we're working against it. We want so badly for the violence against women to stop. We have to hope, otherwise there is no point in continuing to help.

EYE: When was the happiest time of your life?

MAMAN: In my life I was happiest when I was with my grandmother. I was so happy because she was so old, and I saw her and asked myself, *Can I, too, live that long?*

EYE: Thanks, Maman. Your strength and courage to continue working to help others even during the most horrific times are an inspiration. We thank you for your heart, your compassion and your will to keep fighting.

First published in July, 2011.

Part IV:
Helping the Forgotten

"In a gentle way, you can shake the world."

—*Mahatma Ghandi,*
Spiritual and Political Leader

Tina Hovsepian

Tina Hovsepian on Ending Homelessness with Cardborigami Shelters

By Patricia Caso

Architect Tina Hovsepian is quickly becoming a godsend for the homeless, globally. When I saw her unique design of a portable cardboard home based on origami, the ancient art of paper folding, I was fascinated by the simplicity and genius behind it.

> **"Cardborigami provides a jumpstart for someone who doesn't have much. It provides privacy, which you and I take for granted."** *—Tina Hovsepian*

Tina calls her shelter Cardborigami. It's also the name of her proactive organization for transitioning one homeless person at a time off the streets. People from Nepal and 92 different countries are already interested in obtaining and learning more about Tina's invention.

Tina took some valuable time out from her schedule in Los Angeles to speak with me about her visionary ideas...

EYE: What does a portable shelter mean to a homeless person?

TINA: In addition to providing a safe space, there is a psychological aspect of it. A person has ownership of something that is useful and looks nice. Cardborigami provides a jumpstart for someone who doesn't have much. It provides privacy, which you and I take for granted.

Even if the homeless go into a shelter or program, there are usually beds in a big room. Again, they are exposed to the public or everyone around them. Finally, this shelter is aesthetically pleasing which is meant to be uplifting, supporting the idea of feeling better about oneself.

EYE: How is it better than a tent?

TINA: There is no assembly required. There is initial construction but that is done on the front end. Once you get it, you simply pull it open and it's ready to go. It's sturdier than a tent, but weighs only 20 pounds.

> The cardboard provides structural stability and the folding patterns increase the stability. It loads better and it's a little more insulated than a tent.

Instead of a layer of plastic, it has little air gaps inherent in the cardboard material, providing a little bit of insulation. That means it's warmer inside when it's cooler outside, and cooler inside when it's warmer outside.

Cardboard is protection between you and the "floor." It's all treated to be really good at resisting water, making it last a lot longer than regular cardboard if there is moisture or mold.

EYE: Have you spent a night or two in it yourself?

TINA: Volunteers, board members and I spent a night at Sleep Out To End Homelessness in Venice Beach. It was to point out how laws against people sleeping in their cars were ridiculous since they have no place to go or sleep.

We gave out shelters to some of the homeless people. That night was really cold and it was sprinkling. One woman got so warm in her Cardborigami that she had to take off her jacket.

The feedback on the shelter and the personal street stories were important to me there and when we visited Skid Row several times.

EYE: Is there a limit to how many times Cardborigami can be opened and closed?

TINA: We know for sure we can open and close it 40 times. For my standards that is not a lot, but I've been told that *is* a lot for what is needed in a disaster situation.

Because these are transitional shelters, we don't want people to live in them for too long; we want to have them in permanent places in 10 to 12 months. These should last 10 months. Ideally we don't want them to have to.

EYE: You've said this is not meant to be a handout. How does the overall program work?

TINA: Cardborigami's goal is ending homelessness or filling some gaps. We partner with organizations that have connections, and facilities where the shelters can be used safely.

Once someone has gone through Cardborigami's four-step program, they will be in a position to navigate society on their own.

(1) People use Cardborigami on safe property.
(2) Our organization will get people access to social services they need.
(3) Permanent housing is obtained through vouchers and other available methods.

(4) People can keep their houses through employment. We will hire people to assemble the shelters, partnering with entrepreneurship programs or other job placement organizations.

EYE: What intrigues you about the homeless that got you started?

TINA: I grew up in L.A., which has been dubbed a U.S. capital for homelessness. I constantly saw the negative reactions toward the homeless. People would ignore them, or they would take a step back if they tried to talk to you. As a kid I would ask why it was this way.

The main inspiration for doing something about it happened when I traveled around Southeast Asia, stopping in Cambodia with my architecture program at the University of Southern California. We visited an elementary school, which we were supposed to redesign, and also visited the surrounding village.

The conditions stunned me. Their lives were in such a stark contrast to my own—and I'm not really wealthy either. I told myself to start appreciating things more.

Right then I decided to give back. If I am so privileged, then it is my responsibility to give back. The very next semester at the University of Southern California, I had my project assignment and I designed the Cardborigami structure.

EYE: Is there an inspiration for your structure?

TINA: I was really influenced by Shigeru Ban, [an architect] who builds everything out of paper. Waterproof and fire-proof qualities are important when you are building permanent structures.

EYE: How did you finance this?

TINA: One Cardborigami structure costs $30. Because of design awards, prize money and publicity, I tapped into different networks, social media and networking opportunities, and then met people who believed in how this could help.

People are reaching out to me with financing. We had a lot of original small donors, and we continue to get grants from companies like Annenberg and Toyota.

EYE: You also have a day job at Callison, a premier architecture firm. What are you working on now?

TINA: I am working on designing the expansion of a new wing in the biggest outdoor mall in the U.S.

in the Ala Moana Shopping Center in Hawaii. The man hired me at this wonderful firm because of my Cardborigami project, and the firm has supported my efforts in so many ways. In fact, employees helped me build 20 shelters.

EYE: What kind of architecture intrigues you?

TINA: I like super-small, intimate things that are easy to understand, like Cardborigami. I am even more interested in large, mixed-use buildings. In the ideal sustainable organization of the future, there would be huge developments built around transportation hubs.

It's not only a sustainable way of living, but also the buildings and materials would be sustainable.

How to generate energy with buildings is another major interest of mine. I am really geared to the future and how to make the world a better place.

EYE: What do see in your future?

TINA: I want Cardborigami to be a sustainable organization, even without me. Having that under my belt, I would like to be a successful architect, designing environmentally sustainable and socially responsible buildings.

Most built environments are built by developers, not by architects. I want that to change. I envision making housing that pays for itself and that looks good, not only for homeless to transition into, but for people in general to live in, so there would be ideal social integration.

EYE: It is my understanding that requests for Cardborigami come from as far away as Nepal.

TINA: Yes. That happened the day after I spoke at the Women in the World event in New York. Through Twitter and social media, many people said that would be a perfect solution for all the crumbled houses because of the recent earthquake.

Through a connection with a Nepalese foundation, we are now participating in a UN Habitat Mission. So I will be going to Nepal mid-June to early July.

I will be setting up useful mapping instruments to identify vulnerable households in troubled regions. I'll also develop a monsoon impact map.

I personally will extend my stay, visit the manufacturer in China and import Cardborigami shelters where they are needed.

EYE: Do you see a commercial use for these shelters as well?

TINA: There are many applications, from shelters for people in Syria and Iraq who have no home at all to a children's toy or camping shelter and so on. The profits from the commercial side will be used to help fund the nonprofit activity.

EYE: I read your description of yourself: "architect + social entrepreneur / extraordinary + at least half crazy." Explain!

TINA: I really believe when you are in the trenches, you must get loose, get crazy, laugh and then get back to work. There is a saying that "there is no genius without madness." I have experienced that I guess!

EYE: As Tina noted at one point in our conversation, homelessness can happen to anyone. Much success to you, Tina, as you increase awareness for the homeless and continue to innovate beyond Cardborigami.

First published in June, 2015.

Dr. Roseanna Means (left) and a client
in Boston, Massachusetts

Dr. Roseanna Means
Goes Beyond Medicine
to Help Homeless Women

By Patricia Caso

I was intrigued by a *CBS Evening News* report on Dr. Roseanna Means, which depicted how she brought healthcare, and more, to the vulnerable on the streets of Boston, Massachusetts. In 1999 she founded the Women of Means organization (now called Health Care Without Walls), a nonprofit that helps homeless women and children.

Dr. Means and her group work in seven shelters and often right on the streets, logging in 8,000 to 10,000 patient "visits" each year.

> "I didn't insist they give me their real names. I don't wear fancy clothes or a white coat. They call me Dr. Roseanna. I am always there on the same day, same time, predictable, comfortable and very approachable." — *Dr. Roseanna Means*

Perhaps because she has experienced double knee replacement, melanoma, divorce and a new marriage, Dr. Means can more easily diagnose these women. As I learned, this selfless, inspiring doctor and her team do much more than practice medicine...

EYE: What do you see when you work with homeless women?

DR. MEANS: I see courage. These women lose all their material possessions, even their children and their relationships. There are a myriad of indignities that happen when you are poor, when your circumstances change, when you can't think straight, speak up or advocate for yourself. Yet, when women lose all this, I am always so impressed by their perseverance, how they endure.

I've seen these women just beaten down by the system and the social situation, and yet, they come to the shelter ready to help out their friends, remember somebody's birthday. They will tell a good joke. They put their hand on mine when I am having a tough day. We have no idea what it's like for these women to go through what they go through.

> Yet, their ability to transcend their situation, embrace the human condition, be able to give back and join humanity is quite

remarkable under the circumstances. I just love these women!

EYE: What myths of homelessness have you found?

DR. MEANS: Stereotypes like homeless women are all bag ladies, lazy, talking to themselves, ranting and raving on the streets, etc. Situations like that are really quite rare. The majority of these women have bad luck more than they have mental illness. They've been abandoned by a mate, or divorced or their husbands died and they lost everything.

Some raised their kids and never got a job. Or, they had a part-time job on the side with no benefits, and then a horrendous medical calamity came along and they could not pay their bills. Some of these women are just remarkable people, not bad people at all; they did not let things slide.

Things happen to them, time runs out and there they are, living on the streets. Importantly, many of the women we take care of are not homeless anymore. These women move on.

EYE: How do you gain the trust of these women?

DR. MEANS: I listen a lot. I pass no judgment. I try to find out what I can do to help. I meet them where they are. In the beginning, I found that going in as a goody-goody with my blood pressure cuff and stethoscope, I wasn't able to reach women who had been assaulted in the past.

If you are working with a woman who has been assaulted or held down and you put a blood pressure cuff on their arm and pump it, it feels like bondage to them, which is very, very scary to someone who has been physically traumatized. So I learned podiatry.

I offered my services to women who didn't want me to get too physically close to them. I would sit on the floor, put their feet in my lap, cut toe nails, shave calluses, give them a foot massage and keep a conversation going. Sooner or later they would open up. It wasn't so scary for them.

I didn't insist that they give me their real names. I don't wear fancy clothes or a white coat. They call me Dr. Roseanna. I am always there on the same day, same time, predictable, comfortable and very approachable.

EYE: Is social justice something you always aspired to?

DR. MEANS: I grew up in the Boston area and my mother encouraged me to give back at an early age. I am one of these children of the '60s who were influenced by the Kennedys and very much tied to the saying: "To whom much is given, much is expected."

No matter what your position in life is, you should always think about giving back! At 13 I started as a candy striper. In high school, I spent a summer in Appalachia helping in the coal mining community.

When I got past a dark time in my life that involved divorce and double knee replacement, I decided to give myself a present by going to Nepal to work with kids in orphanages and do some climbing. That's who I am.

EYE: What prompted you to take action and start Women of Means?

DR. MEANS: I found that homeless women were not coming into the government's homeless clinic for a variety of reasons. I became aware that we have 75-year-old women sleeping on the streets of Boston in the wintertime. Little kids who have an ear infection or a tummy ache were staying in a hotel room or in a family shelter literally for years on end. I thought this is just outrageous.

This is not something we should accept as the

wallpaper of our society. So I decided to do something with absolutely zero skill other than my own innate talent, skills and training. I didn't know how to write a grant, ask for money, navigate labor laws, hire people, etc.

Over the last 15 years, I've learned a lot by doing, trial and error, and I've been enormously blessed with amazing workers. Many doctors who volunteer for a year have stayed five and ten years.

EYE: Is there a pivotal moment for your decision to make this work your mission?

DR. MEANS: I was a medical resident at Brigham and Women's Hospital when I took three months off to work at the Cambodian border with the refugees. On arrival, I told them I didn't know their language or cultural beliefs, and had not experienced what they'd been through—genocide.

But, I was there to do what I could to help. That was a very powerful lesson for me as a young, impressionable doctor. I had gone to MIT, then medical school and was lined up to be a cardiologist, a lucrative career.

> I returned from Cambodia with the decision that I needed to do something that would make a mark in people's lives.

I saw the Cambodian people, who had been through a nightmare, and there they were singing, teaching their children the cultural dances, how to make baskets and the language.

> **I felt really privileged to witness that enormous resiliency. I was able to take that in and incorporate it into a way of life, a way of professionally dealing with people for the next three decades.**

EYE: Switching gears, why are you are climbing Mt. Kilimanjaro? You must be a very capable athlete.

DR. MEANS: Either that, or foolhardy. I was not athletic until college where I rowed crew. When I got my knees replaced, I had to learn how to walk and climb again. Kilimanjaro was one of those mountains I always wanted to climb. One day I was talking to someone and said without thinking, "Being homeless is harder than people realize. There is a mountain of obstacles to overcome just to keep going."

And then it clicked—that I was facing a real-life mountain only once, and these women face a mountain every day. I thought, "If they can do that, I should take strength from them and get myself to the top of Mt. Kilimanjaro to honor the struggles they are enduring day after day." I asked our supporters to join me in solidarity on this climb by donating to Women of Means to help us keep our programs going.

> **Sometimes it feels like I am at the base of a 20,000 foot mountain and I don't even know where to put my first step.**

EYE: What is your daily life like?

DR. MEANS: My life is a balance of different competing interests. My full-time job is running Women of Means, basically their chief cook and bottle washer. My "half-time" job is being the primary care physician for a group of patients at the Brigham and Women's Hospital, where I've been on the medical staff for 32 years.

Then I have my three grown sons with whom I try to meet on a regular basis. And, not the least is my husband, my second husband. We got married last year. I wake up between 4:30 and 5 a.m. and don't get to bed before 10 p.m.

EYE: Do you ever feel like your commitments are too big?

DR. MEANS: I have moments when I wonder, *What the heck am I doing?* Yet, I am surrounded by so many people who are on the same page as I am, in terms of the social justice of this. This is why Women of Means is very possible and important.

EYE: You were a 2011 CNN Hero featured on network news and in print articles. What do you want from all this media attention?

DR. MEANS: It's not about me; it's about who the women are. There, but for the grace of God, go any of us. Hopefully, awareness will bring in donations, making Women of Means self-sustaining as well. We have no government money and no fee-for-service model.

We are based on volunteerism. Literally, we change lives, save lives and give the women the *means* to move forward with their lives.

EYE: You must know you are an inspiration to so many. Is there anyone who has inspired you?

DR. MEANS: Yes, one of my first patients, Cheryl. I met her 20 years ago when she was homeless and helped get her housing. At that point I diagnosed her ovarian cancer. She backed out of surgery three times because she was so scared. She then got breast cancer, but survived.

She's taught me a lot about homelessness, human dignity, what it is like to be in the street and how the system beats you down. Her resiliency really inspired me. Whenever I've had my dark moments and I've thought, *You have to be crazy to be doing all this with the skills you have*, I would think of Cheryl.

I cannot let her down. She's been through so much. She's taught me so much. She's been my mentor. She's shown me what it's like for these women and I have to do it, keep doing it, for her.

EYE: Thank you, Dr. Means, for this inspiring look into your remarkable life. We will be following your progress with great interest. All the best to you!

First published in June, 2013.

Doniece Sandoval

Doniece Sandoval's Lava Mae Brings Showers and Dignity to the Homeless

By Patricia Caso

Homelessness is a complex issue and a major concern in a growing number of cities around the world. Like many, I have donated clothes and given money to agencies and organizations. San Francisco's Doniece Sandoval went much further and came up with a way to bring dignity to the homeless, "one shower at a time."

> "I thought, *If you can put gourmet food on wheels and take it anywhere, why not showers and toilets?* So the idea for Lava Mae was born!"   —*Doniece Sandoval*

She's done it by retrofitting a bus and naming it Lava Mae, a twist on the Spanish words for "wash me." Doniece does not purport to end homelessness, but rather to make a small but significant difference in the lives of the overlooked.

After speaking with Doniece, I was inspired to find out about her motivation and how Lava Mae came to be. I think you will be inspired, too!...

EYE: How did this innovative idea come to you?

DONIECE: We moved from New York to San Francisco in 2002. With my adopted three-month-old daughter, I would stroll the neighborhood and got to know many people. After the downturn, our neighborhood became trendy; gentrification set in. Too many of our neighbors moved from their homes, to their cars, to the streets.

It's been heartbreaking. We felt powerless to help, and I wanted to figure out some way to make a difference. I could not put my head around how you end homelessness. It just seemed so complex.

One day I was walking in another neighborhood and I passed a young woman sitting on the sidewalk. She was crying, filthy and muttering to herself that she would never be clean.

EYE: Was she the reason you decided to take action?

DOENICE: Yes! I knew she meant a lot of things by those words that I would never understand. I wondered what her chances were of getting physically clean. That evening I did some research. There are more than 7,000 homeless in the city.

About half of those people live on the streets near shelters that don't have showers.

> So, upwards of 3,500 people on the streets have to make do with the seven drop-in centers that have showers. That's 14 shower stalls for 3,500 people! I thought that was utterly criminal.

At the same time the whole mobile food craze was going strong. I thought, *If you can put gourmet food on wheels and take it anywhere, why not showers and toilets?* So the idea for Lava Mae was born!

EYE: Who was your first call?

DONIECE: I called Jennifer Friedenbach, who is with the Coalition on Homelessness in San Francisco. It's one of the oldest and most venerable advocacy groups for the homeless in the city. She would be my litmus test.

I heard she's tough, and she's smart. I was pretty terrified. I thought her attitude might be "Who *are* you? You've never worked with the homeless." Not that at all.

She started pulling out information for me, information on public health, the impact of not having access to showers, the number of bug bite visits to San Francisco General Hospital, etc. She said, "Yes, if you can do this, GO! This is awesome!"

EYE: I understand that you went without a shower for a full week so that you could experience what many homeless go through?

DONIECE: My friends were teasing me that I was doing a publicity stunt because my background is in marketing and public relations. When you are in the middle of a crowdfunding campaign, you have to do things that capture people's attention.

But the lion's share of that was the idea of stepping into people's shoes and struggling to stay clean for a week. Of course I had a completely illusory sense of homelessness, coming home every night and sleeping in my warm comfortable bed.

I am a bit of a clean freak, so it was a challenge for me not to take a bath, step in a shower and fully wipe the day's grime off. I tried to pop into the bathroom in my office or use the wipes in the bathroom in the local grocery store to clean myself off.

But it left me with the impression of just spreading the grime around, rather than actually cleaning myself up. I was certainly not feeling good about myself.

EYE: Were there any surprises from this experience?

DONIECE: I think one of the things that surprised me about the people who knew what I was doing was that they would say, "Oh yeah, you're not showering! How's that going? You look great! You don't look dirty at all. You look perfectly clean."

What hit me was that we have a really strong perception that stems from the superficial about what people are doing, or what state they are in, based on how they look. It's not always accurate. But on day six, I walked into the kitchen and my six-year-old daughter said, "What smells?" I knew it must be me.

> When I finally got to shower, about a minute into the water hitting me, I started to cry. I realized that part of me had disconnected and shut down. Being in a shower felt warm, protective and restorative. It was a very emotional experience.

EYE: This is a complex project, two years in development. Were you prepared to navigate all the issues?

DONIECE: The only experience I had with the homeless was volunteering with different organizations throughout the years. I don't think I quite knew what I was undertaking. It's like that saying, *What you don't know might be better for you. If you know everything, you might not do it.*

I started by knocking on doors of nonprofits to find out if this was even a reasonable idea. I thought they would say one of two things: that this is crazy and I should just go away, or that this is so brilliant; we want to do this! I don't think I expected that I would be the person executing it as well.

> **What I did find was nonprofits who said: *You are crazy and we want you to do this and we'll help however we can.* So I knew if it were going to happen, then it had to be up to me.**

EYE: How do people sign up and what can they expect?

DONIECE: Our partner nonprofit drop-in centers get the word out and people sign up for Lava Mae at their site. That way people don't clog up the sidewalk or waste their own time waiting in line.

We get them when it's their shower time, orient them, and get their towels and toiletries for a 20-minute appointment and 10 minutes of hot water for their showers. So far everyone has been very respectful and we tweak the time when someone is disabled, taking extra time getting on and off the bus and in and out of the shower.

We are starting slowly to do things really well. Thirty showers a day is realistic in a five-hour period.

EYE: Have you found any resistance in the neighborhoods?

DONIECE: Sadly, a little bit. However, the majority of the people in the Mission District are very supportive. They see the benefits for all the people involved and are happy to see us there.

EYE: I read that each bus cost $75,000 to fit Lava Mae's needs. How did you come up with the money? Can you sustain this with all the maintenance, etc.?

DONIECE: We launched our effort for Lava Mae on a crowdfunding site, Indiegogo, raising $58,000. The rest came through our website, all from just regular people who thought this was a really great idea.

EYE: What have you learned from your initial participants?

DONIECE: We showered 20 people in our test run.

Silas was our first. He is from the South, a charmer; he loves to have his picture taken. He almost kissed our feet because he had this opportunity.

In getting to know him, one learns that he meanders around the city because he was cited by police for sleeping on a bench. Silas is always looking for a soup kitchen for lunch. He relates this without pity or bitterness.

> Silas is working to stay clean and loves the opera, even managing to get tickets. You have got to love him. There are no words for what it means to connect with a human being in this way and feel you are just a small part of making his and others' lives a little bit better.

EYE: What are some of the challenging issues you've had to face?

DONIECE: One of the scariest times was finding the company that would retrofit the bus. To no avail, I called companies all around the country who do promotional tours, work with rock stars, etc. Ultimately, we found Airco, a local company that basically builds the guts for skyscrapers, who were more than thrilled to accept the challenge.

Another was to include the wheelchair radius in the bathroom floor plan, which is completely ADA-compliant. We need to serve the disabled, who are 46% of the homeless population. Then there were little things like the water from the showerhead that splashed so the toilet paper roll got completely saturated.

EYE: How do you reflect on this whole project so far?

DONIECE: I am driven to be creative and productive. Until Lava Mae, I was like Lucy in the *Peanuts* strip. I'd love to have a pop-up booth like she did, and have people pay me to just come up with good ideas, because I am good at that.

In my time here in Silicon Valley where creativity abounds, I've learned that ideas are cheap. A lot of people have great ideas. Executing them is, at the end of the day, what really matters.

It's hard. It's a lot of work. On a broader level, we need to change nonprofits. There needs to be some blending of the private sector mentality—the startup engine kind of mentality—with nonprofits so that nonprofits can be better, stronger and more resilient.

EYE: How have you gotten through the tough challenges without walking away?

DONIECE: Until I started to get a staff, it was my husband who supported this project since day one. He believed in me and my ability to pull people together to make this happen.

Second, I may have had the idea and gotten the ball rolling, but so many people have come together. I really feel like we've built a village to make Lava Mae happen. It didn't happen just because of me. That has sustained me over and over again.

EYE: We hope that Lava Mae continues to grow and expands to many cities. As you believe, access to showers and toilets should not be a luxury; it's a basic human right. Thank you, Doniece!

First published in March, 2014.

Part V:
Advocating for Special Causes

"We must have perseverance and above all
confidence in ourselves. We must believe
that we are gifted for something."

—*Madame Curie,*
Nobel Prize-Winning Physicist

Jane Heller

Novelist Jane Heller on Finding Humor in Caregiving

By Stacey Gualandi

New York Times bestselling author Jane Heller took a slight detour from her romantic comedies to bring us a new caregiver's survival guide called *You'd Better Not Die or I'll Kill You*.

> **"I think we all need to have certain guides to lead us. We don't have a manual for raising kids or caring for our elderly parents. So that's what I wanted this book to be."** **—*Jane Heller***

Jane started out as a publicist, promoting authors. Now, thirteen very humorous romantic comedies later, she is an acclaimed author herself. After reading her guide, I am amazed at how she has kept her sense of humor while being her husband's caregiver for many years.

You can tell by the title of her book that Jane is certainly not letting the stress and strain get her down completely. She recently shared some valuable tips and a new outlook on caregiving with me in this excerpt of our interview on *The Women's Eye Radio Show...*

EYE: Were there a lot of rejected titles, because this was a really good one?

JANE: No. Actually this is the first thing that popped into my mind, because I wanted to set the tone that this is not going to be a Debbie Downer book. But, also, it is literally what I say to my husband, Michael, every time he goes into surgery.

When they'd wheel him up on the gurney to the double doors for the operating room, there he'd be and the nurse would say, "This is where you have to say your good-byes." And I would lean down and wag my finger and say, "You'd better not die or I'll kill you." And he would laugh and off he'd go.

I always thought that was better—sending him off with a smile—than having him see me all weepy and nervous. So that became the title for the book.

EYE: It really works well because it takes a bit of the edge and the stress off. It's that little moment of levity that puts everybody at ease.

JANE: I think humor helps, period. It certainly keeps me balanced. There are situations that are not funny, and I, in no way, want to be trivializing or dismissive of what caregivers go through.

I think there are times when we have to step back and say, *You know, this is absurd and if I can't laugh at it, well then I'm sunk.*

EYE: It's probably what's gotten you through this for so many years, too. If it was all doom and gloom for the whole time, your health could really have been negatively affected. You might not have stayed in there for the long haul.

JANE: That's right. We caregivers do have to take care of ourselves. So many of us neglect our own health because we feel that it's self-indulgent to take time away from caring for our loved one. That couldn't be further from the truth because if we can't be healthy enough to do it, who's going to?

EYE: This is your fifteenth book, including your previous nonfiction one. You are your best promotional expert because this is how you started out, promoting other authors—people like Erica Jong and Judy Blume. Being an author wasn't something you ever thought was going to be your destiny, right?

JANE: This is true. In fact, I was raised by a mother who cared for two sick husbands. My father died of cancer when I was six, and then she married my stepfather, who ended up dying of complications from epilepsy.

I said to myself, *Some people marry for money and some people marry for looks; I'm going to marry for health. I've seen too many men drop dead in my life, and I'm going to marry a man without a medical flaw.*

Well, the joke was on me. There is no such thing. We are thrust into the role because nobody knows what the future holds, so I became one of the 65 million or so caregivers in America. We say the vows "in sickness and in health" when we stand there at the altar. I don't know that in the throes of passion anybody pays a whole lot of attention to that part of the vow.

EYE: So many of your books are romantic novels with the Jane Heller light-hearted flair. But this book, while it's a nonfiction guide, is a romantic story, too, because it's the story about you and your husband. Underneath all of it, is this really a love story?

JANE: You have to really love somebody to go through some of the things we have. We just celebrated our twentieth anniversary, and it's been a bumpy ride!

When you're talking about spousal care-giving, it really is important to make sure that the person you're caring for doesn't feel like they are a burden.

I write about the power of touch and how important it is to touch the person you're caring for so they don't feel like a burden.

I interviewed a critical care nurse in our hospital here, and she said that some people come and visit their loved one in the hospital and they sit in that visitor's chair and read the newspaper. They forget to get up and give the person a massage or hold their hand or just touch them.

EYE: Your husband has Crohn's disease. How has that affected your life?

JANE: Crohn's is an autoimmune disease. It affects the digestive system. In the same way that arthritis or lupus attacks the joints, Crohn's hits you right in the gut. Michael was diagnosed at age 11, and he had many surgeries because the intestines become inflamed. It's a chronic illness, so it's never going to go away.

It has to be managed with different medications, some of which cause their own problems, which create personality changes and a lot of things I talk about in the book. But when I met him he was in remission so he fooled me.

When he mentioned that he had something called Crohn's disease, I said, "Well, what's that?" I'd never heard of it. He said, "It's no big deal and don't worry because I'm fine right now."

> Then, shortly before we married, he had his first trip to the ER, and I thought, *This is not no big deal.* But nearly a hundred hospitalizations later, here we are.

EYE: Unbelievable! This is something I went through when my dad was dealing with cancer; I wish that I had this book with me. There are so many things people are not going to know about until they get to that point.

JANE: Right. I wanted to tell people if you're feeling this, it's normal. I think that we all need to feel that we're not alone, and so I just wanted to have chapters that said things like *Crying is not a bad thing in small doses; it's important to eat a meal; you're not being self-indulgent if you actually take time away; and go out with a friend and enjoy yourself.*

I think we all need to have certain guides to lead us. We don't have a manual for raising kids or caring for our elderly parents. So that's what I wanted this book to be.

EYE: I think another thing that's really important— and this is something I told my mom as she was going through it with my dad—is that while you're caring for someone else, do not neglect yourself. This was something that you didn't talk about until writing this book. Is this your big coming out?

JANE: I would say that. I did neglect my health because I thought, *How can I take time to go to the doctor? I'll just wait.* So you end up putting off things, and that's not a good thing.

You don't sleep; you don't eat. In 2010, Michael was in the hospital four times, having had two surgeries. I don't think I took a breath that whole time.

It was a rough year; I suffered the consequences. A big message to people: Don't neglect your own health. Even if it feels like it's not the right thing to do, you need to do it.

EYE: It was very important for you not only to share your own story but also to interview other people who are caregivers, and also professionals in this field. How did you go about getting someone like actress Linda Dano, actor Victor Garber and others to be in your book?

JANE: Once you put the word out that you're looking for people who have gone through the caregiving experience, it's quite easy. I wanted to cover the spectrum, whether it's someone dealing with Alzheimer's, as Linda and Victor did; or Harriet Brown, who talks about her daughter's battle with anorexia; or Yudi Bennett, who talks about her son who's autistic.

Whatever the circumstance, even though the specifics are different, we all go through the same emotional experiences, and I wanted to make that point.

I wanted to have my roundtable of caregivers share issues like how they got sleep when they had trouble sleeping, how they dealt with doctors, how they exercised. I wanted to know whether spiritual care was important to them.

I didn't want it to just be my story. I wanted to throw it out for all to contribute. Then I wanted to seek out experts in a variety of fields—from a dietitian to a therapist, a meditation teacher and even a cookbook author with recipes for those of us who say, "Who has time to cook?"

EYE: Yes, you've got recipes and exercises in this book as well. You've covered every ounce of what it means to be a caregiver. How does your husband feel about all of this?

JANE: It's funny. People ask him how he feels about being so exposed in the book because certainly it's very warts-and-all. At first I gave him the manuscript and I said, "Look, if there's anything in here that you're uncomfortable with, it comes out."

He read it and there were a couple of things that he didn't feel great about. Then he said, "If it'll help somebody else, leave them in." He's definitely a keeper.

EYE: An important thing you talk about, too, is caregiver burnout. How do you deal with that?

JANE: Make sure that you exercise and take time away. I talk about creating a mental vacation. If you can't get away, hop on a plane mentally and do all that stuff that way.

My escape of choice happens to be the Food Network. I can turn that on and watch any of those chefs cooking and I forget everything. We all have our escapes, and I think we need them.

EYE: Is it important for caregivers to have a list of silver linings?

JANE: Yes, because we can get very dark and think very low. It's important to always try to literally make a list and ask yourself what are the bonuses that I have that I didn't know I would have.

EYE: Jane, thank you so much. You've written a very helpful book for anybody who needs it, and there certainly are a lot of us who do.

Originally published in April, 2013.

Sukey Forbes

Author Sukey Forbes on Finding Life After the Death of Her Daughter

By Patricia Caso

Sukey Forbes struggled mightily in dealing with any parent's unimaginable nightmare, the sudden death of her six-year-old daughter. Charlotte had a rare genetic disease, malignant hypothermia. Her body could not cool itself down.

> **"I am really conscious every day of all the gifts small and large in our relationships. You get a real appreciation for what's important when you are laid bare by unexpected hard times."** — *Sukey Forbes*

In Sukey's memoir, *The Angel In My Pocket—A Story of Love, Loss and Life After Death*, she candidly and movingly addresses her process of grief. After reading her book and speaking with Sukey, I found not only a very comforting and instructive way of handling grief but also of handling life when the rug is pulled out from under us...

EYE: Tell us about your daughter, Charlotte, and what life was like with her.

SUKEY: Charlotte was a middle child of three, full of personality. She really ruled the roost, dragging her older brother and younger sister around on all sorts of misadventures.

Charlotte was this lovely little blonde child with a devilish smile and big green eyes. She always had this little sardonic grin, always looking for the humor in things.

She had a great sense of fun and the absurd, very adventurous. Yet, Charlotte was absolutely a girl's girl. She loved every princess out there and loved dressing up.

EYE: What made you feel so stuck after Charlotte died? How did you come to grips with her death?

SUKEY: I was stuck in the maternal instinct of needing to know where she was. It was as if you're at a park and you lose your child. I was frantic, and I could not access my own grief until I had a sense of her physical location and her soul. That superseded anything.

I kept asking so many people, "Where is she?" like a character out of a Gothic novel in an existential crisis. Shortly after Charlotte died, someone I knew sent me a letter recounting a friend's near-death experience.

He had a glimpse of the afterlife in the presence of what he describes as "God," a beautiful white light and acceptance. He didn't want to come back. For some reason that shifted the tide.

> **I clung to that evidence that Charlotte was in that clearly good place. That was enough to set me on my path and quiet me down a little bit. I could settle into myself at that point, start to feel and process.**

EYE: Where did you find the strength to proceed and still care for your other two children and husband?

SUKEY: That's where I drew my strength. I thought that the only thing worse than losing a child would be if my surviving children lost their childhood as a result of that. Similarly, I was married to their father and I needed to be there for him, as he needed to be there for me.

EYE: You kept a journal throughout this whole process. Why was that such an effective tool in your grieving and healing?

SUKEY: I have always been a journal keeper. Writing for me is the way of making sense of what is going on inside of me and out. And, for me, sitting quietly with the exercise of putting pen to paper frees up my thinking.

> I would add journaling as one of my top recommendations for anyone whose life has taken an unexpected turn, not just for people who are grieving. Writing is a very powerful vehicle. Many of the answers to the questions that burn in us are deep inside of us.

We just have to sit quietly, write, and they will come out on the page. If we spend too much time looking outward and not examining inside we won't have the ability to get those answers.

EYE: Mediums and clairvoyants figured in your process as well. How are you so comfortable with the spirit world?

SUKEY: We grew up in large old houses. There was a sense of spirits or ghosts. Many of my family members have personal ghost stories of some kind. While I didn't give a whole lot of thought to the presence of ghosts, I just sort of generally believed that there was more than just concrete life and death.

When Charlotte died, I was placed in that position of having our life take an unexpected turn, and I didn't know how to proceed. When I began to look outside of myself for answers, I was very open-minded. We need to look inside in equal parts to looking outside of ourselves. And if we do too much of either, we get stuck.

This became a turning point for me. Henry James refers to it as an absorbing errand. He wrote, "True happiness, we are told, consists of getting out of one's self...and to stay out you must have some absorbing errand." Clairvoyants and mediums may not be the answer for others, but for me they resonated.

> It gave me in very concrete terms a validation that life and death are just steps along the continuum. Our loved ones are separated from us, but not gone.

EYE: Will you explain how going to a medium gave you the final assurance that Charlotte was okay?

SUKEY: In the medium's guided meditation, we got in an elevator and went several levels. For me it opened up onto a very broad field like the one Julie Andrews was on in *The Sound of Music*. It was a beautiful green grassy area and then from far, far away I saw Charlotte.

In an instant Charlotte was about an inch from my face shaking her head back and forth saying, "Hi Mummy! Hi Mummy! Hi Mummy!" in a playful sing-song way. I just knew that this was not my imagination. It was her.

It just felt so concretely that it was she who was visiting me. She was so okay! It was as if you picked up your child from a wonderful day at school and she came, threw her arms around you and said she had the best day and went on and on.

I began to weep. I was physically exhausted, puddling to the floor with relief, physically overwhelmed. I knew she was okay and accessible.

EYE: What do you mean "accessible?"

SUKEY: I feel very much that in times of quiet, in times of need, if I sit quietly and think about her, very similar to praying, she is like an angel or higher being who is hearing and helping and guiding on the other side. Charlotte is accessible.

EYE: The philosopher and poet Ralph Waldo Emerson had a lot to do with your process. He also is your great-great-great grandfather. How was he so integral in helping you?

SUKEY: He was important to me initially as a family member, not as a poet or the sage of comfort. When Charlotte died, I looked to my family first for a sense of the structure of how they had handled loss.

Ralph Waldo Emerson had lost his six-year-old son to a fever. I lost my six-year-old daughter to a fever, so that felt to me like a very powerful connection.

I was aware that Emerson's last words were, "That boy. That beautiful boy." That had always haunted me and been curious to me. He was a seeker. He had lots of questions. He went to his wife's crypt a year after she died, opened the door, and said, "I just had to see."

> I identified with that desire to have more understanding of what had happened, what had become of the flesh and blood. I came upon his quote, "Sorrow makes us all children again, destroys all differences of intellect. The wisest know nothing."

I thought, *Oh, my gosh, we all do become children again when we are stripped emotionally from loss; we have to find our way again emotionally and build ourselves back up.*

Emerson also wrote about self-reliance, God's presence in nature and the divinity inside each one of us. Those are family beliefs I grew up with.

He also described his fears and inability to feel. "I chiefly grieve that I cannot grieve." There were a lot of parallels that kept circling me back to him as a strong force in my own life.

EYE: What did you find were the most important steps in your healing?

SUKEY: Writing, for sure. Next, open-mindedness to other ways of thinking, a general curiosity to explore other possibilities. Our natural inclination is to circle in when we are in pain.

Opening our hearts and minds, which is very hard to do, is critical to the healing process. I am also a big believer in reading to discover a potential path. After that would be physical movement.

Grief and emotion store themselves inside our body at the cellular level. We can't think and feel our way through grief; we have to move it, literally move it through our system. I was very aware of being unable to take a full breath. I still feel that tightening at emotional times. Exercise and movement can move pain and emotion out of the body.

EYE: Was there an obvious obstacle to your healing as you look back?

SUKEY: I was afraid I would never emerge. Had I known more that this was a process I would move through, that I could be okay and be a better person if I wanted to, then it would have been easier to slide into that abyss for awhile.

We all have times when we feel awful. We feel like it will be endless. But I was so fearful of falling off that cliff and never landing, never emerging, that made it very difficult to process.

EYE: Why did you ultimately write a memoir about such a personal tragedy and struggle?

SUKEY: We need more examples of people who are resilient, who are courageous about moving through it and writing about it. The grief is part of the story, but it is the ending that sets it apart.

I want people to take away the comfortable resting spot. We all get there in

different ways, yet there are common ways to get through it.

People cannot put their noses to the grindstone and ignore the pain. Like Winston Churchill said, "When you are going through hell, keep on going." We do get through it if we want to. That is the message in my book.

EYE: What personally surprised you on the other side of this process?

SUKEY: I am a much better person having gone through this, although I didn't dislike myself before. My heart has grown; my capacity for curiosity and empathy and understanding is greater. My life is richer and more abundant in all directions.

I am really conscious every day of all the gifts small and large in our relationships. You get a real appreciation for what's important when you are laid bare by unexpected hard times. I will say that I would give all that up in a nanosecond if I could have my daughter back. But I can't bargain her back, much as I'd like to.

So, I am deeply appreciative of the wisdom and the capacity of being a human being that I've gotten out of the process. I am happy.

EYE: Thank you for making time to share lessons from your personal loss with me, Sukey. Certainly there will be many people who will benefit from your memoir.

First published in July, 2014.

Lauren Daniels

How Lauren Daniels HEALS Families with Cancer

By Catherine Anaya

Lauren Daniels is one of the most wonderful women I have had the pleasure of meeting. At age 35 she was told she had breast cancer. That diagnosis changed the direction of her life.

> **"I was very fortunate. Other people had $100,000 worth of medical bills. So we decided that we wanted to provide hope to some of these moms as they were going through this."** —*Lauren Daniels*

She saw the tremendous need to help moms and their families who were dealing with the challenges and the expenses of cancer just as she was. Lauren is truly healing through her organization HEAL— Happily Ever After League—in the home she calls Healing House.

Lauren and HEAL give one of the most creative and fun fundraising teas you could ever imagine— the Fairytale Tea—once a year to raise money for the nonprofit. It was such an honor to have her as a guest with me on *The Women's Eye Radio Show...*

EYE: You founded HEAL after you were diagnosed with cancer. How did you come up with that name?

LAUREN: It actually came to me in a dream. I knew I wanted to start a foundation with an uplifting name. Everything I kept thinking of sounded like it was a retirement home. It just wasn't working for me.

One morning I woke up and the words "happily ever after" kept ringing in my head. I thought *What does that mean?* Maybe it's "Happily Ever After Foundation?" I've lived happily ever after since my cancer diagnosis and others can as well. We came up with Happily Ever After League and it spelled the word "heal" and it's worked for us beautifully.

EYE: And perfectly! You had a family history of cancer. I remember you told me that getting cancer wasn't a surprise for you because of your family history but getting it at 35 was.

LAUREN: My mother has had breast cancer twice. So it wasn't the furthest from my mind, thinking that at some point in my lifetime I would have to cross that path. I was never expecting it right after my third child was born.

The results of tests came out positive and I was having to deal with this and with three kids ranging in age from 1 through 11. It was not something I was looking forward to.

But I had seen family members who had triumphed through it so I knew I could handle it. With the support of my family, I was really able to get through.

EYE: You mentioned three children, one as young as one. How difficult is it to battle cancer and try to be a mom at the same time?

LAUREN: For me, I was fortunate. I did not have to go through chemotherapy because I caught my cancer so early. But, I did have to have three surgeries in a four-month span of time. I always say that for a mom to have a common cold is a luxury.

You cannot take the time to take off and rest and recuperate from just a cold, let alone the time that's needed to recover from chemotherapy or radiation or surgeries. It's necessary to wake up every day and be there for the family.

My priority was to be able to still be there for the kids and be positive. Everyone seems to take mom's lead. There would be days I'd cry in the shower, but when they were all looking up at me, I was trying to forge on.

EYE: That is not easy. You help women who are dealing with any type of cancer, not just breast cancer. What led you to say to yourself, "I need to do something for women who are going through this who have a family who needs that support?"

LAUREN: I had been hearing that women were taking the city bus to the breast cancer surgery. I found out that women couldn't afford the medications they needed to get the treatment they needed. Even though we had very good insurance, we still had to pay $4,000 out-of-pocket that year and pay it off over time.

And yet, I was very fortunate. Other people had $100,000 worth of medical bills. So we decided that we wanted to provide hope to some of these moms as they were going through this.

EYE: In your first fundraiser, you raised $50,000! That's pretty impressive.

LAUREN: We did. About six months after my diagnosis, I decided this was what I was going to do. Those who know me best said, "This is a great idea! Do you think you should wait a bit longer?"

But my parents, my husband and all of
my good friends knew that once I make
my mind up, I'm going to do this. So we
can either get on board or just get out
of her way.

On the one-year anniversary of my diagnosis was
when we had the fundraiser. In the room was "six
degrees of Lauren," I'm sure. Everyone knew me in
one way, shape or form.

And we did; we raised $50,000! We were in
business. We were able to start giving out grants to
the moms who needed it. At the time we were
helping out with rent, utility bills, etc. and that has
evolved over time.

EYE: How do you determine whom you help? Is
there a process?

LAUREN: There is a process and we do have an
online application. They have to be in active cancer
treatment. They need to have a least one dependent
child living at home. Aside from that, as long as they
qualify and we ask for a list of their doctors and
that type of thing, we are able to get a one-time
grant and they can start using our Healing House.

EYE: Do you work with healthcare providers in
identifying some of those women?

LAUREN: Mainly we do. We work with social workers and a lot of oncologists' offices. We've found that the moms we've helped are sharing our resource with other mothers. There's a lot of word of mouth.

EYE: What kinds of support are you able to give them? Obviously you are not able to pay their entire medical bill. But, every little bit helps, doesn't it?

LAUREN: Yes, it does. For me, as founder, it is important that we give the most that we can. For a long time I struggled with how great the need really was. Knowing what we were able to give, it was not going to be able to solve all their problems.

> **But what I found was that the gift we gave them and just not hearing "no" and knowing that someone cared just gave them hope to get through another day.**

It empowered them to know that there was a community behind them that really cared. The ongoing support that comes from the Healing House is something that helps them along the way.

EYE: Healing House is an actual house. What I love about it is that it is not just about the woman going through cancer, but it is about her entire family.

LAUREN: That is definitely the case. Our focus is that we help the mom but the entire family unit is affected. We do help dads and caretakers and children because the house is there as a reprieve for families.

> **They need time away socially and to have a fun day with people who know what they are going through. They don't necessarily need to talk about cancer.**

Clearly, we all know that's why we're there. We call it a "cancer free zone" because we focus on living, not necessarily on cancer.

EYE: I imagine you get very attached to families and the women who are going through cancer, in particular. Not everyone survives. How difficult is that for you?

LAUREN: It's one of the things I found to be most challenging. It is my belief that these moms are living happily ever after in a different place. But we do get attached.

When we don't hear back from them, especially when we know that they were struggling, we chat about it and hope they are doing okay. It is definitely very difficult for me, having walked through a cancer diagnosis. It just never gets easier.

I have to make it okay in my head. I hate to say it but I have to treat it "businesslike" and try to get to a place where I can continue to do this work and not hang up after every call and cry and be upset.

I need to continue to be strong so that we can continue to provide this very needed resource for these moms.

EYE: You've expanded beyond Phoenix to Atlanta. How did that all come about?

LAUREN: One HEAL mom's mom would come in from Atlanta to help her through radiation and chemotherapy. She would come to the Healing House with her. Unbeknownst to her daughter— who would go into the food pantry—her mom and I would chat about her daughter and her recovery.

She would always say, "I cannot believe what you all do. This is so wonderful." She would cry. She'd pull it all together before her daughter returned from the pantry. She said, "I think I want to do this in Atlanta." And I kept saying, "I think you should!"

She did. It's been running for a couple of years. It's on a much smaller scale, but they are still providing help for the women of Georgia.

EYE: Do you see that as part of your vision, having HEAL pop up in various states across the country?

LAUREN: We were certainly very open to it. We used Atlanta as a template to see how we could make that work. We see that it can.

> Arizona is not the only state that would need a resource like this, so I definitely think there can be one in every state in the country. We would certainly be a resource for any place in the country.

EYE: I want to touch on the Fairytale Tea Fundraiser. Unless you actually have been there, you cannot even imagine what transpires from a couple of people putting their heads together, and, of course, a table.

LAUREN: A hostess comes in and she picks a fairytale or a whimsical theme to put together a table and invite ten of her friends. It's almost like a little private party; you invite your friends and it is just such an amazingly uplifting experience.

Last year someone rented a U-Haul to bring their tablescapes into the hotel. From Tarzan to Tinker Bell to *The Three Little Pigs* to *Charlotte's Web*, the room is just amazing.

EYE: Much continued success in all you do, Lauren, especially the Fairytale Tea and the Healing House. It is such a special place.

First published in May, 2016.

Patty Chang Anker

Author Patty Chang Anker Shows "Some Nerve" in Facing Fears

By Stacey Gualandi

Patty Chang Anker, the author of *Some Nerve: Lessons Learned While Becoming Brave*, was facing a big fear when I spoke with her last time. The challenge she faced was learning to ride a bike at the age of 40. She took her own advice, found "some nerve" and was able to conquer that fear and many more.

> "There were a lot of skills that made me highly nervous, so I never practiced. If you don't practice, that is a huge contributing element to fear." —*Patty Chang Anker*

She set out, not just to ride around the block, but also to bike 40 miles through the five boroughs of New York City on the TD Five Boro Bike Tour with 32,000 other riders. Returning to the radio show, she gave me the lowdown on how she did on the demanding course. No training wheels necessary for Patty now...

PATTY: I'm alive! Thank you for your prayers! Your thoughts carried me through the day!

EYE: Yay! Being the author with the title *Some Nerve*, you had to put your pedals where your mouth was, right?

PATTY: It was highly inconvenient for me to have written a book with that in the title, yes! I was approached by Bike New York, which provides free bike lessons to kids and adults across the City.

I had taken their adult Learn To Ride class and my kids took the Kids Learn To Ride class. It was a wonderful experience, which I wrote about in my book. Then I promptly forgot about it until they got in touch with me and asked if I'd be interested in doing a bike tour. And I said, "Whaaaat?"

EYE: Isn't that nice that they remembered you?!

PATTY: I was really busy facing other fears with public speaking and women's self-defense classes, and I really hadn't gotten back on the bike.

EYE: You really had not quite conquered riding a bicycle, had you?

PATTY: I hadn't. I was game with my first lesson, learning how to balance and how to turn and brake. I wasn't too good at getting off the bike. I was better going left than right. There was a lot to work on.

I was scared to go out in the world with other elements, like having other bikes on the path. I was terrified of getting out on the road or having to take a hand off the handlebar to signal.

There were a lot of skills that made me highly nervous, so I never practiced. If you don't practice, that is a huge element of fear.

EYE: You were an expert, having written the book. But you had to be afraid and overcome your own fears to help other people. Did you discover other fears?

PATTY: I think that another underlying fear of mine is the fear of failure or that I won't see something through. In my life, I've quit a lot of things. As soon as it gets discouraging, as soon as I feel like I might fail, I opt out.

> I'd say, "I wasn't cut out for that thing; leave it to other people. I'm not very athletic. It's not my strength; it's a waste of my time."

EYE: Why does that happen?

PATTY: It's just that kind of thinking that can keep

you from pushing through the challenges.

Once you push through them, that's where courage lies, that's where strength gets built. That's where facing yourself comes in.

All the goodies come from working through that, and in the past, that's where I took the signal to quit. On the worst day, I would quit before I began. There were all sorts of things I just wouldn't do.

EYE: If that was your pattern, then what changed for you?

PATTY: What I discovered interviewing people who faced all kinds of fears was the stories we tell ourselves about why we don't do certain things. Whether it's our cultural background, like *I'm Chinese-American and Chinese-Americans aren't very outdoorsy or athletic unless you are training for the Olympics and then we always win gold.*

Then there is the values story, that we place more value on education rather than physical activity so I never developed this as a strength.

EYE: How did you change your mindset?

PATTY: What I learned from hearing this over and over again in regard to swimming or driving or fear of proposing a toast is that we think we have reasons, but they are actually just stories we tell about why we hold ourselves back.

Open yourself up to saying, "I am capable of growing, changing," and allow yourself ups and downs.

I literally crashed a couple of days before the bike tour. I was going too slow. All my fears were that I would be going too fast, going downhill and out of control and creating a terrible crash.

I was actually pedaling uphill into my own driveway! It was humiliating. One of my teammates said if your pedals are no longer moving, your feet should no longer be on them. Crashes happen. You may get hurt. It just is the way life is. So, you can't let that stop you.

EYE: I understand you had a team that joined you on this bike endeavor.

PATTY: Yes, Team #SomeNerve. It was amazing. More than 40 people joined from across the country. There were a number of riders who did not know anyone. I think that takes a lot of nerve. Over half the team had never done the Five Boro Bike Tour before.

There were several people who worried that they would not finish—me, prime among them. It was a huge sense of accomplishment. Everyone who set out to finish, finished. The feeling at the end was incredible.

EYE: Tell me about this tour. How long did you prepare for it? Were you fearful up until you crossed the starting line?

PATTY: I was fearful all the way to the finish line. Are you kidding me? You are talking to a woman who has so many fears, she wrote a book about it. The fear did not stop.

I think that was a huge lesson in life too. The fears don't stop. If you are someone who naturally worries about things, a lot of enjoying life is to be able to navigate that.

I actually declared this challenge around New Year's Day in January. It was a May Tour, and I bought my bike in February.

At that point, I could not bike around the block. I tried a test run on my new bike, and I had to get off. I was weeping. I was going down hill and there was a car that was trying to parallel park and there was intersecting traffic. I was so overwhelmed that I almost quit right there.

EYE: How were you able to continue?

PATTY: What I'll always remember about that was it happened right below the Manhattan Bridge. About eight weeks later, I was doing a training ride over the Manhattan Bridge and my husband called down and said, "Look down, look down! That's the street where you almost quit!"

> **Eight weeks later I was already crossing two bridges—biking 10 miles. The amount of progress one can make when one puts one's mind to it is tremendous.**

EYE: How did you get through with the hand injury you suffered?

PATTY: I had this sense of determination that I'd never felt before. I think that's "some nerve." In the past, if I hurt myself I would have felt, *That's it, I'm not supposed to be doing this. It is a sign from God.*

My doctor said if I injured it again, I could break it. You know what! I could break my good wrist just riding my bike. I couldn't let that stop me.

I wanted to finish, even if meant a little collateral damage. I wanted to go through with it.

EYE: You have scars to prove it now, right?

PATTY: I never understood what that meant before when people would say that, but now I do.

EYE: It probably got worse towards the end. You must have been exhausted.

PATTY: Yes. We had brutal headwinds and I felt like I was moving backwards, not making any progress at all. It's so hard to have any faith in yourself when you are going beyond anything you've ever done before.

A friend riding beside me put his hand on my back for a little boost and that felt so good. I had this encouragement from my team the whole time, which was absolutely critical. Then there was an uphill over "the beast," the Verrazano Bridge.

It's two miles, the longest suspension bridge in America, and it's the end of the tour. After you've been dealing with all these potholes and headwinds, etc., you're going up this on-ramp. By then, I was crying. It was pure exhaustion.

Many people were dropping back to walk their bikes up. I felt like if I got off I would never be able to get back on.

EYE: How did you ever finish?

PATTY: There was all this inspirational writing on the floor of the bridge, "keep cranking, four down, one to go," and U2's "Beautiful Day" was blasting and it was so inspiring. All those thoughts—I can't do it; I'm not good enough; I won't be able to finish—were chasing me and then all of a sudden it leveled off. I'd reached the highest point on the bridge!

One moment you are pedaling as hard as you can and it is so painful, then the next one becomes easier. Then I realized: *I've done it; I am going to finish*. It just erased all those negative thoughts. They were gone because I did it. And it was proof.

> **I think that is the lesson I am going to take with me for the rest of my life for any obstacle. I am able to do more than I think, much more than I think.**

That's the truth. It feels like your past experiences are the truth or your past failures are the truth. The truth lies in your future success.

EYE: What do you want people to take away from your challenging experience?

PATTY: The experience of declaring to do something that is unlike you, not something that you would typically do, something that would surprise people who know you. The value of that is huge. You get to see yourself in a different way. The world gets to see you in a different way.

If anyone were to say, "Patty Chang Anker is sporty," before the last four months, everyone else would say, "How many people are named Patty Chang Anker? She's not the one I know." But you see, I *can* do athletic things.

It's opened up my life and I can enjoy it with my husband and children. It can really add spice to your life and be meaningful in a way that I never anticipated. So, pick the thing that is out of character and see what you learn from it.

EYE: Thank you for joining us. We applaud your ability to expand your universe and to urge others to try new endeavors. I can't wait to take on a big new challenge!

First published in August, 2014.

Advice from Some of our Changemakers on Making a Difference

Barbara Massaad:

To get a program like Soup for Syria started, it takes empathy and an open mind with simple ideas. I would tell people that it is possible to accomplish any project once you put your heart and soul into it. Many people discouraged me from undertaking this project, but I did not listen—and luckily was able to make a difference.

Maggie Doyne:

Spend time in the specific region you are interested in working in. Learn the language. Read, read, read! Gain as much knowledge and facts and figures as possible. Find local partners equally committed and invested with similar ethos, dreams and visions. Start small, with one child, one mosquito net, one meal. We believe that miracles are a result of hard work. So no matter what you do, never ever give up.

Jenny Bowen:

Believe in your dream, be fearless about going to a place where you don't know what's going to happen and realize that perfectly ordinary people can play a part in making the world a better place. Because I felt driven to do this thing, I did something that everybody said was impossible.

Estella Pyfrom:

Write down your dreams. Include your action plan for making your dreams become a reality. Once your vision is clear, put the plans on a vision board or book where you can view daily. Do as much research as possible to find and get expert help. Then begin your positive journey. Work through the "what ifs." Then you will find positive solutions that will propel your project to success

Scarlett Lewis:

Our intentions are pure with no other agenda than to be of service to educators and their students worldwide. I think when you start from that point, everything falls into place. People are attracted to help you in your mission and you find yourself in the right place at the right time. It's helpful when you know you are following your life's purpose and the reason you are here on earth.

Holly Gordon:

Many times it takes enormous determination and courage in the face of fear and uncertainty. Leading is about passion. Don't wait for someone else; stand up and do it if something needs changing.

Tina Hovsepian:

Never give up on your dreams and ideals. Be super-confident. We naturally nurture. We already have what it takes to make the world a better place. We have to be confident enough to do it. Whatever you do is going to be better than what is already out there. Don't be scared. Do it.

Dr. Roseanna Means:

I think that being homeless is harder than people realize. There is a mountain of obstacles to overcome for them just to keep going. These women face a mountain every day. In thinking about the obstacles they have had to overcome, we might all see what strength we can get from them.

Doniece Sandoval:

I'm just one example of the many out there that can make a difference, and it doesn't have to be on this level of big and elaborate. If you feel this calling to help out in your community, don't let that pass you by. Life is too short. It will be something you are proud of and that made your life matter.

Lauren Daniels:

When working towards your goal, listen with your heart and never, ever give up. I also always think of my favorite quote by Edmund Lee: "Surround yourself with the dreamers and the doers, the believers and thinkers, but most of all, surround yourself with those who see the greatness within you, even when you don't see it yourself."

Patty Chang Anker:

I once heard a stoic described as a person who makes a decision once and sticks to it, regardless of what hardships may ensue. Women are often taught to be flexible and accommodating, to assess and reassess decisions balancing the needs of others, and to defer our own goals when kids or parents or significant others need to come first.

What I discovered in facing my fears is that we need to become stoic with the things that matter to us. Our big goal, whether that's to learn to swim or write a book, will be challenging and we'll need all the courage and commitment we have.

Book Club Discussion Questions

1. Which women's stories in this book inspire you and why?

2. What advice do you take from them that would help you achieve your goals or vision?

3. What qualities do these women have that make it possible for them to be changemakers?

4. How do you see yourself making a difference?

5. Is there a particular cause that you want to become a champion for?

6. Would you make that cause your life's work?

7. Are there any roadblocks that would keep you from taking on a big challenge?

8. What kind of a reward would you hope to receive after taking on a cause of your choice?

9. How would it change your life to take on a cause you are passionate about?

10. Has this book inspired you to take any action? If so, what would it be?

Websites for Updates
and
More Information

Part I

1. Jessica Posner (Odede)
http://www.shofco.org

2. Marsha Wallace
https://diningforwomen.org

3. Barbara Massaad
http://soupforsyria.com

4. Paula Gianturco
http://www.paolagianturco.com

Part II

5. Maggie Doyne
http://www.blinknow.org

6. Elissa Montanti
http://www.gmrfchildren.org

7. Jenny Bowen
http://halfthesky.org

8. Estella Pyfrom
http://estellasbrilliantbus.org

9. Scarlett Lewis
http://www.jesselewischooselove.org

Part III

10. Holly Gordon
http://girlrising.com

11. Gulalai Ismail
http://www.awaregirls.org

12. Jerrie Ueberle
https://wafw.org

13. Maman Marie Nozili
no website

Part IV

14. Tina Hovsepian
http://cardborigami.org

15. Dr. Roseanna Means
http://www.healthcarewithoutwalls.org

16. Doniece Sandoval
http://lavamae.org

Part V

17. Jane Heller
http://janeheller.com

18. Sukey Forbes
http://sukeyforbes.com

19. Lauren Daniels
http://www.happilyeverafterleague.org

20. Patty Chang Anker
http://PattyChangAnker.com

Photo Permissions

1. Jessica Posner—Photo: Audrey Hall, Show of Force

2. Marsha Wallace—Photo courtesy Marsha Wallace

3. Barbara Massaad—Photo courtesy Barbara Massaad

4. Paola Gianturco—Photo: Pamela Burke

5. Maggie Doyne—Photo courtesy BlinkNow Foundation

6. Elissa Montanti—Photo: Global Medical Relief Fund (GMRF)

7. Jenny Bowen—Photo: Richard Bowen

8. Estella Pyfrom—Photo: Aaron Zigler

9. Scarlett Lewis—Photo courtesy The Jesse Lewis Choose Love Foundation

10. Holly Gordon—Photo courtesy Girl Rising

11. Gulalai Ismail—Photo: Aware Girls

12. Jerrie Ueberle—Photo courtesy Jerrie Ueberle

13. Maman Marie Nzoli—Photo: Amy Ernst

14. Tina Hovsepian—Photo courtesy Tina Hovsepian and Cardborigami Team

15. Dr. Roseanna Means—Photo courtesy Health Care Without Walls

16. Doniece Sandoval—Photo courtesy Lava Mae

17. Jane Heller—Photo: Michael Forester

18. Sukey Forbes—Photo courtesy Sukey Forbes

19. Lauren Daniels—Photo: Colleen Katz/Pictures in Pixels Photography

20. Patty Chang Anker—Photo courtesy Patty Chang Anker

Books by our Changemakers

1. Jessica Posner and Kennedy Odede—*Find Me Unafraid: Love, Loss and Hope in an African Slum*—Ecco

2. Barbara Abdeni Massaad—*Soup for Syria: Recipes to Celebrate Our Shared Humanity*—Interlink Publishing

3. Paola Gianturco—*Grandmother Power: A Global Phenomenon*—powerHouse Books

4. Elissa Montanti with Jennifer Haupt—*I'll Stand By You: One Woman's Mission to Heal the Children of the World*—Penguin Group (USA) Dutton

5. Jenny Bowen—*Wish You Happy Forever: What Chinese Orphans Taught Me About Moving Mountains*—HarperCollins Publishing

6. Scarlett Lewis with Natasha Stoynoff—*Nurturing Healing Love: A Mother's Journey of Hope & Forgiveness*—Hay House, Inc.

7. Jane Heller—*You'd Better Not Die or I'll Kill You: A Caregiver's Survival Guide to Keeping You in Good Health and Good Spirits*—Chronicle Books

8. Sukey Forbes—*The Angel in My Pocket: A Story of Love, Loss and Life After Death*—Penguin Random House

9. Patty Chang Anker—*Some Nerve: Lessons Learned While Becoming Brave*—Riverhead Books

The Women's Eye Radio Show Hosts

Stacey Gualandi is an Emmy Award-winning

journalist with more than 20 years of experience reporting for local, national and newsmagazine outlets, including *Inside Edition, EXTRA*, Hallmark Channel and KTNV. She has served as host of many entertainment and health & lifestyle programs, and is a contributor to several websites. Stacey is also a certified yoga instructor and a proud mutt mom!

Catherine Anaya is a media personality. She's a

television and radio host, video storyteller, media trainer, motivational speaker, emcee, award-winning columnist, blogger and owner-CEO of 4Hearts Media. The proud mother of two and wife is also a three-time Emmy Award-winning former television news anchor of more than 25 years.

The Editors

Pamela Burke has been a member of the broad-

casting industry and print media for
more than 30 years as a television
executive, bureau chief, producer
and reporter. During that time, she
produced several woman-oriented
television programs including
Attitudes, Working Mother and
*The Working Women's Survival
Hour.* As the founder of *The
Women's Eye Radio Show* and website,
thewomenseye.com, she is dedicated to shining the
light on people around the globe who are making a
difference and changing the world in a positive way.

Patricia Caso was a successful television executive

producer and producer for 15
years. She then freelanced and
volunteered while raising two
young men with her husband,
Laurence. Her interests incude
history, writing, interviewing,
social services and sports.
Since 2012, Patricia has had
the wonderful opportunity to
interview and write for *The Women's Eye.*